To Barb –
Wish it –
Dream it –
Do it!
all the best,
Shelly.

Shelley Walchak

52

Rivers

A woman's fly-fishing journey

52 Rivers

Publisher: 52 Rivers Publishing Company

Copy Editors: Steve Hansen, Carol Oglesby, Carolyn Salmons

Photography: Shelley Walchak, unless otherwise stated

Photo Editing: Shelley Walchak, Rob Schmid

Back Cover Photo: Nick Streit

Art Direction & Design: Gustavo Esquinca

Map Design: Shannon Justis

Printed in China

ISBN Number: 978-0-9906117-0-7

Address all inquiries to:

52 Rivers Publishing Company, Suite 1, 4213 S. Zenobia Street, Denver, Colorado 80236.

http://52rivers.com

For information about discounts on bulk purchases, or to book the author for an engagement, please contact

swalchak@gmail.com

Library of Congress Cataloging-in-Publication
Walchak, Shelley.
     52 rivers : A woman's fly-fishing journey – 1st. ed.
        p. cm.
    ISBN 978-0-990-61170-7 (pb)
    1. Fly fishing. 2. Fly fishing for women. 3. Women fishers. I. Title.
    SH463.P34 2014
    799.1'24'082—dc20

To my father, Robert Brightman, who made it possible for this to happen.

To my husband, Florian Walchak, who is steadfast and loving.

To my children and grandchildren, Scott, Michael, Mike, Megan, Lizzie, Hannah, Ava and Maxwell, who provide the spice of life.

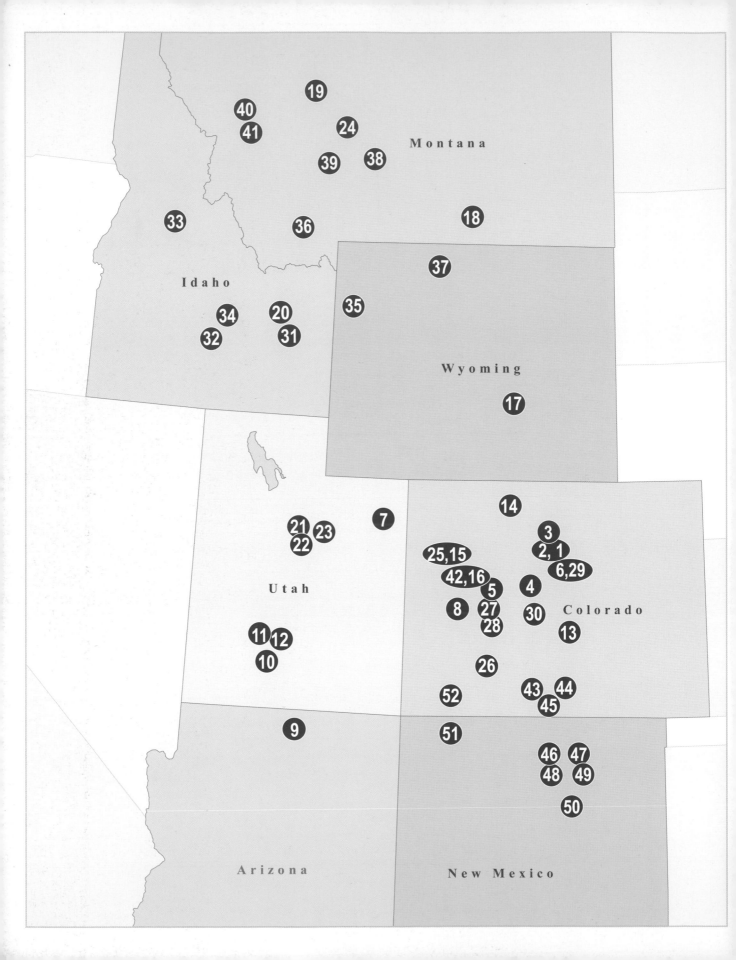

Table of Contents

Acknowledgements

I am grateful for all the patient and knowledgeable guides with whom I fished
and the support and guidance of many people including the following:

My husband, Florian Walchak

My friends, Pat and Carol Ogelsby—the best friends ever

Steve Schweitzer—who encouraged and assisted me with self-publishing

Susan Packard and Jeff Packard

My son, Michael Runyan—who was my biggest fan

And for two companies who sponsored me without my asking: Brothers Flies and Damsel Street.

I want to give special thanks to two friends who served as book editors,
but more importantly encouraged me to continue.

Steve Hansen

I met Steve in 2011 when working on an international conference for librarians in Telluride. His kind and supportive character was apparent to everyone and he was an expert with words and editing. He became a perfect fit in assisting me in the second phase of my journey—telling my story. Steve grew up near the idyllic North River in Massachusetts. He reeled in his first catch (a whopping bluefish) at age 8. When I told him about my idea for *52 Rivers*, he was hooked! He is a community media consultant and lives in New York with his partner, Mike, and their collie companion, Rudyard.

Carol Oglesby

Carol has been an unwavering friend since we met in January 2012. A champion of women's fly fishing education, Carol has conducted classes for women in conjunction with the Western Colorado Fly Fishing Expo and the IFFF (International Federation of Fly Fishers) fly fishing fairs in Idaho and Montana. In 2006 she was honored as Woman Of The Year for the IFFF. Carol has written the Women's Outlook Column for the IFFF Flyfisher magazine for nearly two decades. She has also served as the newsletter editor for her local Trout Unlimited/IFFF Club, Grand Valley Anglers. On top of all that, her fly-fishing skills match her editing skills, which says a lot.

Introduction

I have fallen in love with fly-fishing. My love is mysterious, although not unique. I am driven by a desire to learn everything I can about fly-fishing and determined to spend as many hours as I can near rivers, mountain streams or wherever one can find fish. In one's lifelong search for meaning and connection, I have, like many others before me, discovered a symbiotic relationship with fly-fishing. As famous angler, Joan Wulff stated in her essay in *Sacred Trusts*:

The woods and waters of the outdoors became my church, a place where I could examine my thoughts and feel I was connected to all living things. This feeling is especially strong when, with rod in hand, I am wading a river for trout or salmon...where everything makes sense, where there is nothing but truth. There will be no disenchantment with this church.

In late 2011, I realized it was time to pursue a new direction in my life that would both challenge and reward me in new ways and allow me to spend time alone with my own thoughts and dreams—preferably out in the great outdoors, rather than just gazing at its drama and beauty through office and car windows. Around this time, I also had been thinking about seriously improving my fly-fishing skills after accompanying my angler-savvy husband, Florian, on a couple of fishing trips in the Rockies. Although I loved it, I had a long way to go before I could match his skills on the river. He encouraged me to learn all I could about this addictive combination of

sport, art and sleight of hand, and we both knew it would require time for research, hands-on practice and lots and lots of patience.

Then I came across a most amazing book, *365 Days of Pikes Peak—A Journey*. The book is a collection of stunning photographs of Pikes Peak, documenting the story of that incredible mountain through its changes every day, over one year. After immersing myself in the photos and companion text, the spark of an exciting idea began to form in my imagination that would quickly kindle into a glowing, real-life plan.

I loved the idea of devoting oneself to a project for one year. Why not hit the road and visit different rivers while perfecting my fly-fishing skills? I realized that I couldn't possibly fish 365 different rivers in a year, so, how about a river a week—52 rivers?

Fly-fishing for a year. It sounded too good to be true. How many of us talk about acting on our dreams but never follow through? We imagine spending our retirement years indulging ourselves, but find that our health or some other issue prevents this. My mother fell ill at 62 and never really recovered. I was 62 and determined not to follow in her footsteps.

From the start, I knew this project would be ambitious, but I have never been averse to taking risks in my life. That is not to say I didn't have my doubts. Could I stave off all my family issues for a year? Would I get lonely being in a camper by myself? Would I enjoy fishing for a whole year or was this a passing fancy? Would I miss my lifelong work? Would the rivers all start to feel the same after a while? Would I miss my home and family? How would I take care of flat tires?

All these questions crossed my mind as I worked on the details for the trip, but like Nike's tagline, my modus operandi had always been "Just Do It"! And so, I occupied myself buying and outfitting a camper, purchasing camera equipment, a computer and a new cell phone, gathering research material and figuring out my itinerary. Just work on the logistics I told myself, and make it happen.

I would document my yearlong experience in photographs and share my thoughts and adventures with anyone willing to follow along in a weekly blog, and eventually a book. I decided to focus on fly-fishing rivers in the Rocky Mountains because that's where I fell in love with fishing, and I think it's some of the most beautiful country in the world.

One of the most alluring things about fly-fishing is its complexity. There are so many factors that need to come together in order to become proficient. It's about your rod, how you cast, where you cast, what kind of fly you use at what point on your line, how you tie a knot, the weather conditions, etc. Multitasking in a whole new way! I honestly don't think I could have found a new pastime more perfectly suited to me.

The purpose of this book is to inspire others to pursue their passions. By sharing my story honestly—hilarious flubs, foibles and all—about how I followed my passion to become a better angler, and in the end, a better person, perhaps others will also be inspired to follow their dreams.

Shelley Walchak

August 2014

Chapter 1

The South Platte River at Deckers, Colorado

January 2013

—

Home Waters

—

The South Platte River at Deckers, Colorado

I decided to cut my piscatorial teeth on home waters first—this would allow me more time at home to prepare for the rest of the year since I had retired only two weeks prior to the start of my adventure. In the angling world, "home waters" refers to the river closest to home where you fish the most often. Living in Denver, the logical choice was the South Platte River.

Scheduling a river guide took first priority. I wanted to start my fishing year off with Pat Dorsey, perhaps the most well-known guide on the South Platte, but he fell ill just before my launch. Without any other recommendations, I searched the Internet and stumbled upon Fred Grey, one of the best fishermen I met all year. We arranged a meeting time near the mountain town of Aspen Park, Colorado.

As I climbed into Fred's truck at our meeting spot, I entered into a unique world of maleness. Cigarette ashes were mixed with random food droppings. Used flies decorated the visor and old receipts and clothing shared the floor. Fred personified the rugged, colorful life that oftentimes goes along with devotion to a profession that is more about quality of life than income. With apologies for having a truck with a lot of macho personality, he drove us towards the river past the remains of the Hayman Fire from 2002 and the old South Platte Hotel, which until it closed in 1934, was a regular stop for those going to the mining town of Nighthawk.

I soon found myself in the midst of enormous snow-covered boulders that dominated the stream. What a contrast to my former daily commute to downtown Denver! A gripping feeling of thankfulness overcame me, and I knew that the decision to change the course of my life was right on.

We stopped at one of the many roadside accesses to the river, where I eagerly hopped out of Fred's truck. There wasn't another angler in sight, but the noisy American dippers made their presence known. Even though we had to cope with sub-freezing temperatures, we kept warm from a toasty sun.

Fred rigged up the fishing line on my six-weight Sage VXP emerald-green rod starting with a "thingamabobber" followed by some light split shot and two flies that imitated small underwater nymphs (in simpler terms, a bobber or indicator, some weight and some flies). I had not yet learned the necessary fishing knots (clinch, surgeon's, blood, nail, etc.), so his prowess impressed me. I thought threading a small sewing needle was difficult, but this was much more challenging.

Fred handed me my rod and reiterated the key points: cast your fly to a spot about a foot upriver from the spotted fish, don't drag the fly, lift your rod up gently when you see the indicator go under, keep your tip up, and if the fish eats the fly, be careful not to fight too hard or you could throw the hook. Phew!

"Oh yeah," he added. "A few more things…when you cast, don't forget about the willow thickets along the banks, don't overpower your back cast and be sure not to forward cast too quickly or you'll tangle your line." It's a miracle that anyone ever catches a fish!

As a former librarian, I knew a lot about reading books, but I didn't know anything about "reading" a river. Where exactly did the fish hang out? I quickly learned (obvious to me after thinking about it) that fish inhabit spaces under large tree branches, behind large rocks, or at the edge of rapidly flowing riffles. They flock to these spots to both protect themselves against predators (like me and that hovering red-tail hawk) and to find easy access to insects washed downstream.

The time had come. We stealthily approached the bank, careful not to spook fish that I couldn't see. "See that fish over there?" said Fred pointing at what appeared to be a bunch of rocks a little upstream. Squinting my eyes I took a long look. I wanted to say, "Oh yeah—that rainbow trout just below that brown rock." The truth of the matter was that I saw nothing. Every ten or 20 feet, Fred would spot another fish and the same conversation would ensue. By the end of the day, I probably saw one fish for every ten he pointed out.

Stepping into the river and taking a deep breath, I made my first cast by imagining a clock face where I rotated my rod from 10 to 2. As fate would have it, I promptly caught a branch that overhung the river. With enduring patience, Fred untangled the line and had me step further out into the center of the river.

With the water shallow and the fish wary, I would normally have only a couple chances to make the perfect cast before spooking the fish. On this day, however, the fish excused my awkwardness and let me cast to them numerous times before fleeing. Fred would spot a fish, tell me exactly where to cast, and I would land the flies in the right spot after several tries. Occasionally, I noticed a slight movement of my indicator (or Fred cried out, "Hit it!") set the hook, and in some cases, actually reeled in the fish.

Whether it's the first time or the most recent time catching a fish, the feeling is exhilarating. There is a sense of accomplishment that you have somehow understood all the factors that must come together to make this happen. With

Fred's experienced eye and some decent casts on my part, I ended up catching close to a dozen trout, to my surprise and delight.

As the late afternoon chill beset us, we decided to call it a day. Since I would be returning the next day and wasn't exactly a pro at rigging my line, Fred took my rod but left it intact. We took off our waders and boots, climbed into his truck, and headed upriver to scope out new territory in the land of snow-topped boulders.

We followed the river as far as we could go on a dirt road before it became private. I had seen enough to be excited about returning on my own. Making a few three-point turns, Fred turned his truck around to head home. We followed the curvy road north and I suddenly spotted an object in the middle of the road. It only took a couple seconds to realize it was a fly rod! Fred pulled over as I jumped out to pick it up. As I approached it, I noticed that it was that same emerald-green color as my Sage rod. In fact, it was my rod!

We looked at each other incredulously as we figured out what had happened. After I handed Fred my rod, he had set it down on top of his truck in order to take off his boots and waders. Like many others before him, he had forgotten to put it inside the truck, and drove off. The rod had remained on top of the truck for a couple miles before falling to the middle of the road. Fortunately, we had retraced our steps and found it undamaged. *A bit of good karma spent…*

No life experience would be complete without some drama. It was a good start to the year of 52 rivers.

Chapter 2

The Blue River, Colorado

January 2013

A Reality Check

The Blue River, Colorado

The Blue River in Colorado stretches some 65 miles starting on the western side of the Continental Divide in the Ten Mile Range. In January, most of the Blue River is frozen over. The exceptions are two tailwaters—one below Green Mountain Reservoir and the other below the Dillon Dam. Anglers regularly catch 15-inch rainbow or brown trout in both of these spots.

I hadn't heard the term tailwater until I started fly-fishing. Tailwater refers to a type of fishery located just downstream from a dam. Consistent water temperatures and abundant food sources create ideal water conditions for cold-water fish, such as trout, to thrive. I was grateful for tailwaters because I would have a place to fish in the winter months. Some great information on tailwaters can be found in Wendy and Terry Gunn's book, *50 Best Tailwaters to Fly Fish*.

Fishing the South Platte with Fred Grey was such a blast that I booked him again to guide me on the Blue River. As Fred and I drove the 75 miles from Denver to Silverthorne, we shared stories of big fish, past marriages and life's successes and failures. These topics are also well covered in John Gierach's book, *Sex, Death and Fly-fishing*. As we pulled up to the tailwater below Lake Dillon, I discovered that the river flowed next to an outlet mall. I could find some bargains at the Columbia or Nike outlet store and then walk a few hundred feet and catch a trout!

After I overcame the initial surprise that shoppers rather than deer would be my company for the day, we found a parking spot near the dam. We suited up for a cold but sunny day where the temperature hovered in the low 20s and the wind made it feel ten degrees colder. I had worked hard to find the right clothing for these daylong excursions, including some fingerless gloves that would allow me to partially cover

my hand and still manage my fly rod. I quickly learned that I could not fish effectively with any kind of gloves. I never thought I could tolerate bare hands in the winter, but like an outdoor construction worker, I acclimated. I felt tough!

The river flowed at a very shallow 37 cfs (cubic feet per second). The minimum flow for good fishing on the Blue is considered to be 50 cfs, so we weren't sure what we would find. With shallow water and some newly purchased rose-tinted glasses I thought I would be better able to spot fish. Doesn't the world always seem better through rose-colored glasses? Unfortunately, no. That said, concentrating on the clear, non-riffled pockets of water flowing downstream, it was easier to see *some* of the fish *some* of the time. I started to see shadows in spots that had earlier appeared too shallow to hold these perfectly camouflaged creatures.

Prior to the first couple weeks on the South Platte and the Blue, I fished mostly deep, wide rivers. In those rivers, I had to focus on the "indicator" on my line to see if I could detect a tug that meant a possible strike by a fish. "Indicator" is the fly-fishing world's term for a bobber—a small float placed on a fishing line to hold the hook at the desired depth. Throughout the year my fishing line held many styles of indicators: yarn, thingamabobbers, korkies, hi-vis sighters, and plumbobbers, to name a few.

On the Blue, I didn't need to rely as heavily on the movement of the indicator to determine if the fish had taken my little rojo midge because the depth of the water allowed me to approximate where my flies drifted in the stream. I could actually spot the flash of a fish swimming up to eat them! When the first fish of the day struck, I followed the entire course of its path through the water while reeling it in. I felt like Mme. Cousteau, privy to a world previously unexplored. I cried out in delight, like a child seeing an aquarium in a pet store for the first time.

The beauty of the rainbow trout that we caught astonished me. The distinct black spots covered the fish like a bad case of the measles and the pinkish-salmon colored stripe was distinctive. Not all the rainbow trout I caught throughout the year were as beautiful as the fish we found here.

Before Fred and I headed back down to Denver, we found a local bar and grill and rehashed the day over a burger and some fries. Fred told me that there are few native, wild fish left in the rivers in Colorado. Colorado state fish hatcheries produced most of the fish I caught on the Blue and other rivers I would fish throughout the year. This awareness reminded me of the discovery in my youth of the truth about Santa Claus. Over time, I realized that Christmas still excited me no matter who delivered the gifts. In the same way, there's no better way to get connected to the world around us than standing in the middle of a river catching fish, even if the fish were from a hatchery.

When I returned to the camper that evening, some Internet research pointed to the large number of rivers that have been dammed or altered. Controversial as they are, dams are built to ensure water for our communities during droughts. I found it disturbing that sometimes fish are killed en masse to build dams to accommodate residential water needs. On the other hand, how could I complain about supplying water to communities? Should we continue to build subdivisions if we don't have enough water to supply them? These questions still plague me.

Although I continued to fish near the Dillon Dam that week, I followed the river north to explore some of the other well-known fishing spots like Green Mountain Reservoir. The views were dramatic and the ice that formed in the rivers cast a turquoise blue hue.

Fishing on the Blue changed some of my romantic notions about rivers and fishing. My vision of fly-fishing had been associated with thick pine forests abundant with wildlife including wild fish, raptors, prolific insect hatches and few, if any, people—none of which were the case on this river.

On subsequent days on the river that week, the weather turned cloudy and remained cold. Perhaps the change in weather affected the fish, because I didn't catch another one all week. Most likely it had to do with choosing non-fishy waters, wrong flies, or making a bad cast. No alignment with fish on these days, but I felt aligned with life, which was more important.

The Williams Fork, Colorado

January 2013

Minus 11 and Counting

The Williams Fork, Colorado

I heard over and over again that the Williams Fork River was not fishable in the winter. Nothing was further from the truth. In fact, if I had listened to half the advice that came my way throughout the year I would never have left the comfort of my home in January and February. I was told that river flows in the winter would be too low, the temperature of the water would inhibit the fish from moving to feed—and in the case of the Williams Fork—the mile or so hike to the river would be too difficult. Winter anglers know not to let any of these excuses dissuade them. Without hesitation, I headed out to the Williams Fork.

A local guide and I traveled from Silverthorne, Colorado, over Ute pass, past the Gore Mountain Range and approached the river from the south. We drove through vast, unpopulated country and dodged snowshoe hares scampering across the road. And then we passed a large molybdenum mine—a horrific-looking gash in the middle of the pristine wilderness.

My knowledge of mining operations is deficient and my opinions are based on a miniscule amount of reading; however, the method by which this mine extracts molybdenum is disturbing. Henderson Mine uses the "block caving" method to retrieve its ore. Miners have called this method the "Glory Hole," but not because it's glorious in the traditional meaning of the word. With this process, the ground collapses into a surface depression, creating a large hole in the mountain. The question that remains with me is how do we responsibly use our natural resources and yet be good stewards of the environment? I explored that concept all year trying to find the balance between keeping rivers healthy and using them as resources for our communities.

We set aside discussion on mines and arrived in Parshall, Colorado, to a temperature of 15 degrees but abundant

sunshine. Fortunately no snow had fallen since the last anglers made a pathway of packed snow from the parking lot to the river, a distance of about one mile. As long as our footsteps didn't miss the trodden path, we easily managed the walk. We hiked about 30 minutes, past ranches and dilapidated barns, to get to the confluence of the Colorado and Williams Fork Rivers.

A handsome black lab surprised us as he bounded into the river from the opposite bank to greet us. His dad immediately admonished him, demanding that the lab remain by his side. We skirted the angler, making sure that we didn't disturb his chance for a fish that day.

There were several productive holes to fish in this tailwater about a mile below the dam. My guide tied on a size 22 rojo midge to match the actual insect in the river. I successfully caught a mixture of beautiful rainbow and brown trout, although I failed at my first opportunity to catch a cutthroat, a fish distinguishable by a bright salmon-colored slash on its throat. With more than my share of bad casts and tangled lines, I was grateful for experienced and patient guides who see untangling lines as part of their job description.

In a flash, six hours had passed, and it was time to leave. After the hike in and fishing all day, I realized I needed to muster up some energy to hike the mile back to the parking lot. As we trudged through the foot-deep snow I noticed an abandoned, dilapidated cabin and let my mind wander to the days of our ancestors. How did they have the stamina to cross over mountains, find food, and build shelters to settle this brutal land? They did not have Gore-Tex boots or down jackets or waders to help them ford rivers. Yes, I fished in cold temperatures for six hours that day, but these pioneers dealt with those conditions for winters on end. With this perspective, the hike back seemed relatively simple.

On a subsequent day on the Williams Fork River, I met Mike Kuberski at The Colorado Angler fly shop in Silverthorne. Mike drove us up to the river past the mountain skyline known as Sleeping Indian, south of Kremmling. After passing through Kremmling, we headed east. There were several places to park along the bank next to the mostly frozen Colorado, which we would have to cross to get to the Williams Fork River. We were astonished to see that the river had frozen from the bottom up—something that's known as anchor ice and very rare. I shouldn't have been surprised since the car's dashboard displayed minus 11 degrees when we arrived. We waited in the truck for about 30 minutes until the temperature registered a balmy zero and then decided to give it a try. We headed to the confluence of the two rivers by crossing the ice-covered Colorado. I held onto Mike's forearm because a dip in the river at this time would have ruined the day, to say the least.

Mike brought a videocam that he laced around my back so I could actually prove to my skeptical friends that I could catch fish on this river in January. And catch fish I did—at least a half dozen trout that were happy to be released back into water that was at least 20 degrees warmer than the air. The chemical hand-warmers in my parka pockets helped to thaw my fingers whenever I wasn't holding my rod or reeling in a fish.

Photo by Mike Kuberski

In spite of warnings to the contrary, the decision to fish this river in January had been a good one. It was to be my practice throughout the year to assume the best rather than the worst. I never let the weather scare me away from a trip to a river. I believe that when challenges arise it's important to embrace them. A positive outcome is usually achievable, even if it is totally unexpected. I felt brave and empowered after this experience.

Chapter 4

The Taylor, Colorado

January 2013

A Bit of Insanity

The Taylor, Colorado

When reading a newspaper, I like to check out the coldest and warmest temperatures in my state as well as in the nation. If it's 35 degrees in Denver, it might be -20 in Alamosa, Colorado, or 95 degrees in Miami, Florida. In some ways, this habit enables me to better cope with life. No matter what my current life situation, I can always find examples of situations where I would be better or worse off. I've decided I might as well be okay with what I have.

Gunnison, Colorado, is regularly listed as the coldest place in the contiguous 48 states. Perhaps my decision to fish the Taylor River north of Gunnison the fourth week of January was insane; however, because it is a tailwater, I knew that at least it would not be frozen over.

I drove from Denver along Highway 285 through Bailey and Fairplay. As soon as I approached Buena Vista with the incredible Collegiate Peaks range as its backdrop, I dove right into a raging snowstorm. I cozied up to a snowplow over Monarch Pass, which made for a safe but slow drive.

My fishing partners for the next few days were Carol and Pat Oglesby. I met them in Denver at The Fly Fishing Show in 2012, and we became fast friends. Pat is the President of the Eastern Rocky Mountain Council for the International Federation of Fly Fishers, better known as the IFFF. Carol is a columnist for Fly Fisherman (among many other things). Carol and Pat's support and connections helped me in countless ways throughout the year, but this was to be our weekend to fish together.

We met for a mountain woman breakfast of bacon, eggs, pancakes, and coffee at the local café. The previous day's storm had passed and the sky that morning was deep blue and cloudless. Temperatures hovered in the teens. I was excited to spend the day outside fishing and trying out my new Nikon 7000 DSLR camera.

We headed over to the Gunnison River fly shop for tips from owner, Oscar Marks, on the best flies for the day. There is an unwritten rule that when you visit a fly shop to ask for advice, you help support the business by making some purchases—at least some flies, but preferably some new gadget or apparel that you just have to own. I love this "rule"! I bought a nail knot tool, a new buff (scarf), and a dozen flies. We chatted for a long time, and when we looked at our watches we realized it was already noon. Time to get going.

We took the road toward Crested Butte. The freshly fallen snow blanketed the pine forests and sparkled like diamonds. We arrived at the confluence of the Taylor, East and Gunnison Rivers—aptly named Three Rivers—hung a right, and traveled north towards the Taylor Park Dam. We parked next to the famous "Avalanche Hole" appropriately named for the treeless mountainside across the river.

The plows had piled up the snowfall from the previous night alongside the road, making the approach to the river difficult. Carol and I climbed to the top of the bank and slid down to the river's edge upstream from Avalanche Hole. The fish were very skittish, and after a cast or two they vanished. Navigating the river proved difficult and slow because of the dangerously slippery rocks. Before we knew it, mid-afternoon descended with no fish in our nets.

I waded closer to Avalanche Hole after seeing several fish jump, teasing us to stay a little longer. My fishing friends were not fooled by the pageantry. They returned to the truck and helped me scout for fish from up above. I had to have at least a few more tries now that I was in the heart of the Hole. Those few more casts just prolonged the inevitable. I didn't hook a fish.

When I finally accepted that the fish had outsmarted me, I had to figure out how to get back up to the truck. I could either walk back upstream and ascend the way we descended or blaze my own trail. I opted to blaze a trail since I planned to return the next day.

In waist-deep snow, I plodded back up to the truck. Each step challenged my stamina and thighs. Once on top, I instantly realized my net was snagged on a branch down by the river. Blurting out a graphic expletive, I trekked down to the river and back...we just had to laugh.

Photo by Carol Oglesby

Removing our gear was quite a stiff challenge as our waders were totally frozen from the toes to the knees. We could stand them up on their own as if they were filled with cement, resembling "fisher man-nequins." We stuffed everything in

the back of the truck and warmed up during the ride back to town. We had just enough energy to grab a bite to eat before crashing from the overabundance of mountain air.

The next morning brought more typical Gunnison winter weather—ominous-looking skies and temperatures around zero. Unfortunately, Pat and Carol headed home. After sweet farewells, I drove off watching the weather worsen by the mile. By the time I turned at the confluence, the whiteout started. I knew I should turn around and head home, but I refused to let the weather get the best of me. I wanted to say I caught a fish on the Taylor in January...*call me stubborn.*

I parked in the same spot as the previous day and walked to the leeward side of the car, semi-sheltered from the wind. I worked without gloves to rig up my line. The flies were so tiny and the eyes of the hooks so small I found it nearly impossible to tie on a fly with my frozen fingers. After what seemed like an hour, I managed to rig the line with an indicator, some split shot and two tiny midges.

Grateful to finally put on gloves, at least for a few minutes, I trudged down to the river using yesterday's trodden path. Alongside a nice riffle I made a good cast followed by a good drift. I felt a tug and saw the indicator plunge under water. I cried out with joy. My exuberance was quickly squashed when I discovered that the lower fly had snagged a rock. In spite of being careful about freeing it, I lost it to the river gods.

I needed to tie on another fly, but my hands told me absolutely not, just leave the rig as-is. And so I fished to no avail for the next 20 minutes without even a nibble. I finally succumbed and added another fly, willing to give it one last try. I waded up and down the river, cast in a grid pattern to cover all the water and again, nothing. I finally reconciled that I had to be grateful for the beauty of the falling snow and forget about catching a fish. As soon as I capitulated, a fish jumped twice in front of me as if to challenge me to try once more. But, as Kenny Rogers said, "you got to know when to fold 'em...."

Facing a four-hour drive back to Denver, it made sense to chalk this one up to the challenge of winter fishing. That said, the fish better watch out because the next time I visit the Taylor, I'm going in July!

The Fryingpan, Colorado

February 2013

Panning for Trout

The Fryingpan, Colorado

An air inversion captured the Grand Junction area in a deep freeze, causing bitterly cold temperatures. I kept my eye on the forecast and put off my fishing trip to the Fryingpan as long as I could. In the end, Mother Nature decided I had paid my dues last week on the Taylor and gave me at least a one-day reprieve of 30-degree temperatures.

This was my second trip to the Fryingpan. I fished the "Pan" in December 2012, just before starting my journey and caught the biggest fish I have ever caught—a 27-inch brown trout. I can't actually say I caught the fish because although I hooked it, I asked my guide to help me bring it in because my rig was set up with a size 24 hook (very small) and 6x tippet (thin fishing line), which translates into "very difficult for an amateur to bring in on her own."

I cared more about seeing the fish than bragging about bringing it to the net.

That fish was a jumper, which made it more exciting and more difficult to land at the same time. The finesse that is required to bring in a large fish involves keeping pressure on the line at the same time that you don't yank too hard, pulling the hook out. With the right balance, you direct the fish over to the riverbank, net it, take out the hook, and release the fish back to the river.

My guide skillfully steered it to the bank through the rapidly moving stream. When he reached for the net, we faced a new challenge—it wasn't big enough to hold the fish! I volunteered to race back to the truck from the middle of the river and retrieve a larger net.

A strong current made for a rather precarious situation, especially with fishing boots without studs. I wobbled as I turned to face the bank and grabbed my guide to secure myself. Not a good idea, as I almost brought both of us down. I took a deep breath and slowed down to reach the bank without a dunking. I scrambled up the bank, grabbed the larger net, and made my way back in time to net the brown. The length and bulk of this creature was quite remarkable. Beginner's luck played a large role in this catch. It was a long time before I saw another fish like that.

When I returned six weeks later, I had expectations for more of the same, but that didn't "pan" out. The first relatively warm weather in weeks had brought out a slew of anglers. Driving alongside the river, in the shadow of the magnificent Mount Sopris, we passed one fishing hole after another in search of a spot that wouldn't interfere with another angler's space. We had to be creative.

Like a pony express rider—prevailing through rain or snow—the guide took a back road that had not been plowed the entire winter, or at least it looked that way. Even with four-wheel drive we slipped around until we encountered another dynamic duo of intrepid anglers. In order to avoid blocking their passage, we pulled over to the side of the road and landed in a snowdrift, where the wheels spun futilely, creating a rut. After working on freeing the wheels for 15 minutes, we decided fishing was the better option and left the truck to deal with later.

Finding a productive hole, enhanced by the midday sun, I caught a couple of rainbows—the only fish of the day. We waded up and down this section but again encountered anglers at every turn. I wanted to fish the area just below

Reudi Dam known as the "toilet bowl" because it housed the biggest and largest number of fish on the river, but we didn't have working transportation to get there.

As the sun faded behind the canyon walls, we looked at each other and faced the inevitable—we had to figure out how to get the truck out of its rut. As it turned out, the anglers we encountered earlier approached us to ask for help with a dead battery. One good deed deserved another, and with three strong guys pushing and me at the wheel, we slid our way out of the rut. We jump-started the other car and headed back to town.

The next day brought gray skies, cold and lots of wind. I met up again with my friends Carol and Pat and their friend, Tim Jacobs. Tim is a school teacher and works a fly-fishing summer camp for kids in Michigan every summer. In our own version of tailgating, we told stories, laughed at our foibles, and felt appreciative for friends and life's opportunities. Large snowflakes interrupted our conversation, inspiring us to get in the river.

Mostly, we had the river to ourselves and thought the fish would, therefore, be very interested in our carefully chosen flies. I was meticulous setting up my line and thought I would have fish fighting for my fly, but cast after cast found nothing. Before long, I heard Carol shouting "Yahoo!" catching the first fish of the day in a riffle that followed a bend in the stream. I fished upstream in another riffle but didn't see any action. Distracted by the gently falling snow, I reminisced about my childhood when we couldn't wait to play outside during a snowstorm. I watched the snowflakes fall on the sleeve of my jacket trying to distinguish the various patterns. I felt overwhelmingly grateful for this year of passion, friends and fishing.

As usual, the day passed much too quickly. It was time for a good meal and some sangrias. Off to one of the best local restaurants I have ever discovered—Heather's Savory Pies and Tapas Bar in Basalt. We spent twice the normal time just trying to decide what we wanted because everything looked delicious. When the steaming soup and warm bread arrived followed by homemade chicken potpies and vegetable lasagna, we reckoned that we ended a perfect day even more perfectly.

Chapter 6

The South Platte River at Cheesman Canyon, Colorado

February 2013

A Partnership with the Moment

The South Platte River at Cheesman Canyon, Colorado

The Cheesman Canyon section of the South Platte River, just upriver from Deckers (see Chapter 1), is a world-class fishery. I heard epic stories about the beauty of this canyon and the bounty of its river. I was also told that in order to reach the canyon, anglers must hike a mile and a half through the forest and then drop down to the river. I wondered what that would be like wearing waders and fishing boots.

Stories about the health of the river abounded. The Hayman Fire in 2001 burned out of control in the forests surrounding the South Platte, and then flash floods deposited ash, soot and debris, choking the river. Was I just a little too green for this challenging river?

To top it off, I was going to be fishing with one of the experts, if not the expert on the South Platte, Pat Dorsey. Pat authored several books, but his *Fly-Fishing Guide to the South Platte River* is exceptional. (Pat has been fishing the South Platte since 1980.)

So, with those things on my mind, Pat and I met in Aspen Park, Colorado, and drove the 30 minutes or so down to the trailhead. As it turned out, we were able to meander lazily through the forest, deep in conversation, before we dropped down to the river on a very manageable path. The river sparkled and twisted among the red-tinted willows and newly fallen snow covered the tops of the boulders in a magnificent scene.

With the banks of the river still semi-frozen, we had to be careful not to plunge into the river after stepping on a weak slab of ice. Stopping at the first honey-hole, Pat tied on a typical winter nymphing rig. I think I surprised him (and myself even more) by catching a fish on my first cast. I wondered how many times that would happen this year!

While you are on the river, the rest of life rarely interferes. Perhaps this is the reason I was drawn to fly-fishing. The last couple of years had presented several challenges including children's divorces, lost daughters-in-law, and deaths of elderly family members. At work I turned too many grandiose ideas into self-imposed projects that were difficult to manage for many reasons. But on the river, I found a partnership with the moment. I focused on the river, casting, and watching my line for signs of fish. I didn't think about my challenges or for that matter, chemical warfare, the latest Federal Reserve policy or politics. Here, life was simple.

Pat and I meandered alongside the river and strategized about how to get the really big fish that hung out in the nearly impossible-to-reach pockets. There was one humongous boulder where we spotted an enormous brown trout. "Oh, let's give it a try!" I said playfully. The cast would have

to be perfect in order to catch the current and realistically present the flies. After all, this fish hadn't grown large without being somewhat wise to anglers' antics.

Miracle of miracles! A perfect cast fooled the old fish! The tip of my rod looked as if it would break as the fish fought to win. The lack of strength in my right shoulder, due to rotator cuff surgery just nine months earlier, required an awkward leverage of the rod on my hip. I persevered, swaying my rod side to side applying just the right amount of pressure so the line wouldn't break. Remnants of a beaver dam bordered the bottom section of the hole and it didn't take long for the fish to get the better of me. Just when I thought I had it close enough to scoop into the net, I felt and heard my line zing from the reel. Pat yelled, "Don't let him get under the sticks!" But, it was too late. I lost him to the labyrinth of the beaver hut.

Wading downstream, we encountered barbed wire blocking the river. The Wigwam Club, owners of the next stretch of land, posted several "No Trespassing" signs on a barbed-wire fence that crossed the river. We would need to head back upriver. My uncle was part owner of a private club that owns three miles on the Colorado River east of Kremmling. I did fish there once (and was skunked), and I've also paid to fish other private waters in the Rockies. To me, it's kind of like first class seats on an airplane. Has the rare occasion happened that I've been upgraded? Yes. Have I appreciated the extra service I received? Yes. Do I feel comfortable with being singled out to receive this special treatment? Not really.

I feel the same way about rivers, except even more so. Why shouldn't everyone have access to our rivers everywhere, unless the fish are endangered or the stream needs improvements? In Colorado, landowners own the land under the water, so unless you can float the water, you're not allowed to wade through without permission. Other states, like Montana and Washington, have dealt with this differently. I really bristle when I see barbed wire across a river. Technically, you are not allowed to put an obstacle across a river to prevent floaters, so I didn't understand the allowance of this obstruction. Why am I complaining? Anglers have over 20 million acres of public lands to fish in Colorado. On the other hand, it doesn't seem right to privatize our rivers inhibiting some from opportunities we all should enjoy.

Pat and I parted company, and unbeknownst to either of us, we would fish together during the summer on the Black Canyon of the Gunnison—he to get photographs for his next book, and me to do the same—for my first book! A beautiful sunset topped off my day during the drive back to Denver.

Since Cheesman is only an hour from my house, I returned a couple months later when the snow had mostly melted. I spent a day photographing and inhaling the beauty that surrounded me. I really like the fact that you have to hike to this section of the river because it limits the number of anglers to those who must put forth some effort. In a way, it feels like first-class seats, without having to pay for them or feel privileged.

Chapter 7

The Green River at Flaming Gorge, Utah

February 2013

—

On My Own

—

The Green River at Flaming Gorge, Utah

Family members gave me a grand sendoff as I headed west from Denver on a two-month trip in my new 13-foot Scamp trailer. The confused looks on my granddaughters' (Ava and Hannah) faces were priceless. What are you doing and where are you going in that little dollhouse? They were not the only ones to ask me this question. I was, however, quite clear about what I was doing, where I was going, and why I was doing it.

The learning curve for camper management had been steep, but I felt confident as I edged the Scamp from my driveway over the curb. I had practiced electrical hook-ups, putting stabilizers in place, lighting the hot water heater, hooking up water, working with propane tanks and most importantly, safely hooking up the camper to the hitch. I was confident I wouldn't have a run-away trailer. My destination was Dutch John, Utah, normally a seven-hour drive from Denver, where I would fish the Green River.

Within a couple hours, I faced a snowstorm as I approached the mountain passes near Winter Park, Colorado. I have New York City roots and driving slowly is not something that's in my blood. I've had to give myself many mental transfusions to learn how to drive slowly. Going over a slippery pass with a trailer provided just the incentive. Instead of the normal six-hour drive to Vernal, Utah, it took closer to nine.

The road from Vernal to Dutch John climbed via switchbacks spanning breathtaking vistas of the Uintah Mountain Range to the south. Roadside signs dotted the landscape marking the various geological periods such as the Pennsylvanian and the Pleistocene.

The folks at Flaming Gorge Resort had waited up to show me to my camper spot, which they had kindly shoveled free of snow. Nighttime was descending quickly, but I didn't think I would have any problem backing into my site and setting up the camper before dark. I had packed a bottle of Two Vines Cabernet-Merlot and stashed some vanilla-scented candles to celebrate my first night on the road.

Anyone who has ever tried to back up a trailer or boat behind a vehicle will hear the same advice—just turn your wheel in the opposite direction of where you are aiming to go. Ha! That advice was correct, but contrary to everything I have learned about driving. It was as difficult as a right-handed person trying to write with their left hand. If someone had videotaped me, I would have won a spot on America's Funniest Home Videos. After two-dozen attempts to maneuver the camper to just the right spot so I could plug into the electrical outlet but not run into the post that it was attached to, I began to unload the Jeep.

I opened the door to my camper. The stuff that had been strategically arranged in my cupboards was splayed everywhere including a gallon water jug that had fallen and cracked open leaving its contents on the throw rugs and floor...so much for wine and candles. After an hour of cleanup in ten-degree weather, I laid my weary body down on the bed that I had the foresight to make before leaving Denver and zonked out.

The next morning, I met my guide, Charlie Card, at the fly-shop at Flaming Gorge Resort. Charlie heads up the northeastern Utah operation for the fresh-water fisheries conservation group, Trout Unlimited (TU). Trout Unlimited members and employees are river saviors. Charlie has been hard at work trying to prevent the "Millions" pipeline project from diverting huge amounts of water from the Green River

In the early morning hours, writing and organizational tasks took precedence. Around midday, en route to the river, I couldn't help but shoot some photographs of the gorgeous scenery. By the time I arrived at the parking lot next to the river, it was close to 1:30 p.m., and there was still a lot to accomplish before any fishing could happen. I pulled on my waders and boots; covered my face and hands with sunscreen; searched for my hat; tied on a new leader, a couple nymphs, some weight and an indicator; attached the telephoto lens on my camera; and shoved my net into my wader's belt. With apparatus hanging from my neck and shoulders, my net shoved down my waders and my hands full, I reminded myself of an American tourist abroad.

I had worked hard to understand where fish hang out on a river and thus chose the edge of a riffle. There, fish don't have to fight the fast current, but still have the benefits of oxygen and food being washed downstream. I remained focused for quite some time until some common goldeneye ducks flew overhead, distracting me with their loud, distinct whistling sound. Laying down my rod, I quickly tried to maneuver the camera for the photo opportunity but missed it completely...*OK, back to fishing.*

Unexpectedly, I felt a large tug and watched the indicator zip downstream. Nervous and excited at the same time, I held my ground, careful to keep my rod tip up and my line tight. I landed the 16-inch brown trout in my net with a sigh of contentment. It was a beautiful olive brown, a bit brassy, with yellowish-brown sides and medium-sized red spots. Delicately releasing the hook, I held it by its tail in the river until assured that it wasn't injured and could swim away. This was a moment to remember—my first fish on my own.

The next day I headed south through western Colorado. First stop was Durango, Colorado, followed by the Uncompahgre River, just north of Ridgway, Colorado, and then down to Lee's Ferry near the Grand Canyon to fish the Colorado. I would be fishing with four women on the "Unc" and with my husband Florian at Lee's Ferry. After two months of winter fishing I hoped to find some warmer temperatures...but the "Unc" was not going to cooperate.

to eastern Colorado. Good for you, Charlie. He is also a phenomenal fisherman with the most colorful and organized fly box I have ever seen!

We drove to the river and put in Charlie's beautiful wooden drift boat at the "A" section of the Green just below the Flaming Gorge Dam. The dam dripped icicles from the water leakages, which was evidently just fine! The temperature was in the 30s and the wind was blowing at about 15 mph.

Casting into the wind made for difficult fishing. In spite of that, Charlie knew just the right holes, where I caught lots of rainbow trout that are normally lethargic at that time of year. Charlie indicated that fish in the winter fill up their stomachs once in two weeks, as opposed to fish in their most active state in warmer weather that fill their stomachs twice every day. Just the opposite for me—I want to eat twice as much in the winter.

When you spend a day on the river with someone, your conversation extends beyond fishing and explores the bigger picture of your lives. Charlie and I talked about our upbringing and past and present relationships. I am always amazed to learn about the challenges other people face in their lives. Most of the time I discover how much we all have in common; we are not as unique as we claim to be. How we approach our common challenges is what makes the difference in how well we succeed or not. Are we victims or opportunists?

Charlie related all the interesting tidbits about the river and pointed out several rock formations including one that looked exactly like Snoopy. With rocks, just like clouds, it's fun to look for familiar shapes. The day with Charlie ended way too quickly, but at least I had another day on the river to look forward to. He advised me to fish below "Little Hole" where I would wade by myself.

The Uncompahgre, Colorado

February 2013

Dames and Drinks

The Uncompahgre, Colorado

The drive from Dutch John, Utah, to Durango, Colorado, took me through dramatic country. The road rose and fell in a series of sharp zigzags, and I didn't pass more than a handful of other vehicles on the six-hour drive. The mountains were majestic, snow-covered and stark-looking. My Jeep performed well hauling the little Scamp, and I felt the pull of adventure.

My friend Carol had suggested that we meet up with some of her longtime fishing partners on the Uncompahgre River in Ridgway, Colorado, south of Grand Junction. Eagerly, I drove north over Molas and Red Mountain pass. The sky was blue when I left Durango, but just before Molas Pass, I encountered a Rocky Mountain snowstorm. It was a hairy drive, past old mines and around hairpin curves, so I rejoiced when I pulled into the Paco-chu-puk entrance at Ridgway State Park. I gladly parked my car and relaxed from the tension of high-mountain driving in the snow. The Uncompahgre River unfolded before me flowing from the Ridgway dam, meandering alongside a steep, forested mountainside.

One of the biggest snowstorms of the year hit western Colorado that day, but fortunately everyone endured the drive for this special gathering. I arrived earlier than everyone else and enjoyed a momentary solitude. Interestingly, my kids used to complain that I was never on time. As a child, my sister had been labeled with the moniker, "Miss Never-Ready"—something that made me cringe. I take some responsibility for being late when I raised my children, but I believe that anyone who has served time as a single mother will attest that there are just too many things to do in a day. If completing a chore meant you had to be a few minutes late, so be it. Since I now had the luxury of just looking out for myself, being on time was no longer a problem.

When the four other women arrived, we set our minds to the task—pulling on waders, lacing up boots and rigging up rods. Two feet of snow had already fallen in the area, leaving our surroundings pristinely white and devoid of tracks. No one else in sight, we had the river to ourselves—a five-dame fest! We broke trail down to the river and chose our spots. Within minutes, I heard shouts of, "I got one!" or "Woo hoo!" *Wow! That was quick, I thought to myself. Was I going to be able to hoot out my own victory cry without a guide at my side telling me exactly what to do?*

The day was blustery and cold with snow a constant, but this did not interfere with the fish wanting to eat. We cast into an incredibly productive fishing hole, and it didn't take long before I yelled out, "Fish on!" I managed to net and release it, but my form was comical at best. Normally after a half-dozen (or less) casts into a hole, the fish know that something is afoul and bolt to another spot or ignore the flies. Not on this day. Those fish tasted our smorgasbord of small black midges, hare's ears, rojo midges and soft-hackled flies for hours.

Nancy caught an 18-inch cutbow, a fertile hybrid between a rainbow trout and a cutthroat trout. The most distinctive feature of a cutthroat is the deep salmon-colored slash along the jaw line that looks like a wound. With a cry for assistance to document the beauty and size of the fish, I rushed over with my Canon point-and-shoot only to find that my battery was dead. With a new chest pack stocked full of my latest and greatest equipment, I shoved the camera back into an open pocket and decided to help release the fish with Mary and Phyllis standing by to assist.

As I leaned over to help untangle the fish in the net, the camera plunged into the icy cold water. With as quick a retrieve as I could make, I thrust half my arm (and jacket and long underwear) into the icy water. I could only hope that my camera would survive the dunking. I later used the tried and true method of zip-locking it in a bag of rice to remove all the moisture. One week later, it was back in commission, and all the photos I had taken were still on the SD card. *Amazing.*

We returned to our favorite spots and remained on the river until the late afternoon. Sometimes I focused so intently on my indicator that I forgot to look around me and notice what else was going on. I had a feeling that someone or something had their eyes on me. I turned around in the water and looked downstream to see a stunning heron standing on one leg shivering in the cold.

I didn't think I had a chance to get back to my car, pick up my Nikon and get back to photograph this handsome bird, but I had to try. I kept my head down as if to kowtow to the bird, hoping that would encourage him to stay put. I moved stealthily through the river and reeds up to the bank. When I was out of site of the bird, I ran as fast as I could with waders and fishing boots on through the heavy snow back to the car. I unlocked the car, left my fishing pack on the seat, grabbed my camera, relocked the car with the door lock and headed back to the river. He was still there!

I started taking shots from what I considered a safe distance and then inched my way up by three-foot increments until I got close enough to take some really good images. I finally reached that threatening spot that caused the bird to take flight, but I felt appreciative for how close he let me approach.

Carol watched the scene unfold from a distance and joined me after he flew off. We decided this photo session was a good climax to the day, and taco salads and drinks sounded irresistible at this point. As we approached our cars, I felt a wave of panic as I realized that I had left my keys in my chest pack that was sitting in my locked car.

Thank goodness for roadside assistance. With a single cell phone call describing my whereabouts, I had help on the way within 90 minutes and my keys were retrieved from the inside of my car. So much for the wilderness experience!

My mistake did delay our departure, and I wondered how ditzy these women thought I was—dunking my camera, locking my keys in the car, and unknowingly dropping my net in the river (a story better left untold). To try and redeem myself I bought everyone their first round of drinks that night and convinced the bartender to concoct a new drink that would become the official *52 Rivers* drink, a specially made version of sangria. Talk about creating memories.

52 Rivers Drink:

2½ jiggers red or white wine (your favorite)

2 jiggers cranberry juice

½ jigger Vermouth

½ jigger Tuaca (natural liqueur)

½ jigger raspberry pureé

Fill the glass with available fresh fruit (oranges, lemons, limes, blueberries, pineapple and cherries) and serve with lots of ice. Yum.

Chapter 9

The Colorado at Lee's Ferry, Arizona

March 2013

Enthusiasm Unleashed

The Colorado at Lee's Ferry, Arizona

Lee's Ferry is the start of the Grand Canyon in Arizona. Adventurous river rafters launch their boats from this spot to run the rapids. This spot is so stunning that I find it hard to describe in mere words. As Theodore Roosevelt once said, "The Grand Canyon fills me with awe. It is beyond comparison—beyond description; absolutely unparalleled throughout the wide world."

My enthusiasm about fishing the Colorado River at Lee's Ferry built to a crescendo as I drove by the spectacular scenery in northern Arizona. Like an emotionally charged child, I turned up the volume on the radio, began singing at the top of my lungs and felt overwhelmingly gratified. I loved being able to feel this zeal for fishing and to express my exhilaration. This expressive freedom was particularly sweet to me due to a rather subdued childhood.

As a child, I grew up in a household where children were seen and not heard. I recalled having to curtsey and shake hands with my father's business friends that he brought home after playing golf at the country club. "Nice to meet you, Mr. So and So," I would say. As an adult I compensated for that controlled, restrictive behavior by embracing my feelings and emotions.

I met my husband at the Cliff Dweller's Lodge on the night before our trip. We arose early to meet our guide on time. However, the aroma of breakfast burritos from the motel's excellent restaurant sidetracked us. We spent a little too much time eating and chatting with the young staff, who had signed up for temporary seasonal work so that they could explore the Canyon. It brought back memories of carefree ski-bum days in my early 20s when I worked as a

This was a day of fishing, but it was also a day of connections and stories. It was apparent that we had many things in common. We converged to fish, but also celebrated the goodness of life, hoping our paths would cross again when we parted at the end of the day.

Throughout the day Terry pointed out wildlife, including various species of ducks such as red-breasted mergansers, buffleheads, American coot, common goldeneye, western grebe and gadwall as well as such birds as the common flicker, herons, bald eagles and southwestern willow flycatchers. I later discovered that there are more than 300 species of birds documented in this area.

cashier for a free season ski pass. But wait! I'm living that life again now—albeit fishing not skiing—and with a little more money in my pocket.

At Lee's Ferry, you don't drift down the river in a boat to fish; you take a speedboat upriver where you either fish off the boat or stop, anchor and wade. The first spot where we anchored held lots of fish as long as we made long casts, fed out a lot of line to allow for longer drifts and stripped in the fishing line (as opposed to reeling) when catching a fish. We fished this section of the river most of the morning catching fish in lots of shapes and sizes. Around midday our captain, Natalie Jensen, revved the engine and headed toward a second spot called "two-mile canyon"—another prime location.

After a short lunch break we resumed fishing in this magical spot. At times I found it difficult to focus on an indicator floating in the current with the beauty that surrounded me. However, almost instantly, I had another fish on the line, and this continued for the next several hours; I literally caught dozens of fish. Each time I released a fish into the river, I learned how to handle it more and more gently. I could look into its eyes and feel a momentary connection. "Thank you for this opportunity to meet you and sorry I disturbed you," I said.

The second day on the river was with the Lee's Ferry Anglers' Fly Shop owner and angler extraordinaire, Terry Gunn. When you are with someone who has practiced his craft for 30 years, you know you are with the cream of the crop. You can safely say that he or she has reached that Gladwell metric of doing something 10,000 times in order to be an expert.

At day's end we were close to the Glen Canyon Dam, which is spectacular but not without controversy. The cliffs by the dam house one of the highest concentrations of peregrine falcons in the country. Terry told stories about the ability of these great predators to grab a duck in flight. For all the years he had spent on the river, he had not seen this happen. Just as we rounded the last bend before the dam, we actually saw just what Terry had alluded to—a falcon diving down from its 300-foot perch. At a speed known to be up to 200 miles per hour, he nosedived toward a duck that was flying close to the water. How that duck managed to escape the skilled falcon was unclear to me, but it did. Terry may have to wait another few years.

I left feeling shamelessly exuberant, ready for the next three weeks in Utah.

Chapter 10

The Sevier River, Utah

March 2013

—

Skunked

—

The Sevier River, Utah

I thought it would be difficult to top the week at Lee's Ferry on the Colorado River as I headed north to Utah, but I should have known better. I lived in Park City, Utah, for several years in my early 20s skiing, hiking and partying...and even playing some women's rugby as well! I love Utah. There is something magical, especially in southern Utah, about the beautiful striped sandstone formations, the remote and open canyon country, the slick rock and the steep cliffs.

Serendipity struck prior to my departure from Lee's Ferry when a couple inquired about my Scamp parked outside the motel. I invited them in for a "tour" of the 65 square feet I called home. An extended conversation ensued, covering everything from fishing to woodworking. I discovered they owned a bed and breakfast (Historic Smith Hotel) in Glendale, Utah, close to the KOA where I had planned on parking my trailer. They kindly offered to let me park next to their hotel and use their bathroom facilities and Wi-Fi, and write in an enclosed balcony off the back of the B&B when I wasn't fishing. So, I headed north with a new destination and a story to tell to the caretakers of the B&B when I arrived. The hotel was a gem, but the real bonus was the people I met once I arrived—Bunny, a fellow New Jersey girl and her photographer/writer husband, Jerry.

The first evening I arrived, a massive snowstorm covered most of the Rocky Mountain west with eight to ten inches of snow. It presented a wonderful opportunity for me to hunker down in the camper and catch up on my writing. However, as I tried to focus on putting into words my previous week at Lee's Ferry, I remembered seeing some cedar waxwings the previous evening in the crabapple tree in the front yard. It dawned on me I might have the opportunity of a lifetime to photograph the sleek creatures against a background of fluffy, white snow.

As I opened the camper door the next morning, I heard excited chirps celebrating a bonus food source of dried crabapples. I grabbed my camera and tripod and shot photos for over an hour. When I returned to download them I discovered that the white balance was incorrectly set giving the majority of photos a gray cast. *If you don't first succeed, try, try again.* As I went for round two, Jerry came outside and offered tips on getting rid of the grey with some minor adjustments. I captured the waxwings with the correct camera settings and took some of the best photos I have ever taken. This was one of the priceless moments during my stay in southern Utah.

After two days in Glendale, I arranged to meet my guide on the Sevier River, the first of three rivers that I planned to fish in southwest Utah. The Sevier, pronounced "severe" locally, is the longest river in Utah. As a French major, I still have a hard time pronouncing it the local way, but I guess that is no different than butchering Florida to "Floor–eed–a," which is the pronunciation of a major road in my former home town of Durango, Colorado.

The Tushar and Monroe Mountains served as the backdrop as I travelled past alfalfa fields and reservoirs. The snow-covered mountains rise to 12,000 feet and contain two main watersheds—the Beaver and the Sevier. Due to elevation changes, the mountains are unique in that they support both alpine and sub-alpine vegetation including ponderosa pine, trembling aspen, Gambel oak, as well as pinion-juniper and upland mountain grasslands. I wished I were a botanist so I could have identified all the plant life that surrounded me.

I learned that much of the fishing in southern Utah is on private land. Guides need to develop friendships and trust with local landowners in order to get access to the better fishing waters. My guide, Shawn Saunders, had made all the connections. We started off our day by four-wheeling through private farmland in some pretty quaggy spring mud to get to a stretch of river that looked like no one had ever fished it before. The brown trout population was supposed to be abundant and large, but they decided to play hard-to-get that day, not only at the first hole where we stopped, but also throughout the entire day.

It was a streamer day with the likes of wooly buggers, Galloup's sex dungeons, and sculpzillas. With streamers, I had to fish across and down the stream and then "swim" the fly to imitate a small fish. Just like above ground, the world of rivers has a food chain and a survival of the fittest factor. For some reason, I had a block with this style of fishing and still had not caught a fish using a streamer, in spite of relocating to four different spots on the river.

My first impression about streamer fishing was that it didn't really fall into my vision of fly-fishing. I had read plenty of articles about how line control was easier with streamers, and some actually recommend it as a way to introduce beginners to fly-fishing. It seemed so frantic to me. You constantly cast and strip in line, and I found it tedious. However, it was a way to catch fish, especially bigger ones, because for fish to grow really large—somewhere around the time they reach 15 inches in length—they must switch over to piscivorous creatures.

When you first learn how to do something, you need to be careful about passing judgments too quickly. I saw this often with the elementary students I used to teach. If they didn't understand a new concept fast enough it meant they would fight learning it. It became "too hard" or "boring." I believe this is an outcome of our inability to understand the concept of delay of gratification. As the United States continues to slide in its educational standing throughout the world, I believe we should refocus on teaching our students the value of not giving up by complimenting those students who work the hardest at learning rather than praising those who find that learning comes easy to them. Practicing what I preach, I am not going to give up on streamer fishing until I master it.

Although the fish were nowhere to be found on my days on the Sevier, the other wildlife was constant. Red-tailed hawks traversed the sky, chased away by other birds fearful of them invading their nests. We watched them dive for prey and carry it off for their mid-morning snack. The beaver population had been busy at work as well. The gnawed trees by the riverside banks told the story of their home-building skills. I was tempted to cast to the big fish that hung out near the beaver dams, but would have needed a lot of luck to make a cast that wouldn't snag on the tree limbs.

Southern Utah is not a well-known destination for fly-fishing, but a window exists for good fishing in the spring just after run-off and before the desert heat sets in. The scenery on the rivers and on my extracurricular field trips to Zion and Capitol Reef was unsurpassable. Before I said goodbye to my new friends in Glendale, I spent a few days visiting these National Parks where I hiked through canyons and on slick rock that seemed to sprout juniper plants. The iron oxide, shale and sandstone, uplifted throughout the ages, have outturned colorful cliffs and rock layers that inspire and impress. This is truly remarkable country.

Chapter 11

The Beaver River, Utah

March 2013

Getting it Together

The Beaver River, Utah

My field trip to the Coral Pink Sand Dunes took me in the opposite direction of my next destination, but it was worth the detour. The sea of pink sand I encountered held secrets from the geologic period called Middle Jurassic. Arriving early with my new friend, Bunny, we reveled in the view and the quiet that surrounded us. What we didn't realize was that the park is a popular destination for ATV riders, and it wasn't long before we had company on wheels that changed the ambience. I believe this world should be shared—even with ATVs—and so we enjoyed the scene and blocked out the noise as we hiked and checked out stink bugs.

Afterwards, I drove two hours north to the Beaver Creek campground, in Beaver, Utah, which hadn't officially opened, but since I didn't require the full range of services, the owners allowed me to park there. They opened their seasonal restaurant, Maria's, on the day I arrived, and that meant I had the chance to sample some great Mexican food. The freshly squeezed lemonade in an iced margarita glass was itself worth a visit to southern Utah.

The Beaver River runs 80 miles, rising from the Tushar Mountains and flowing through the town of Beaver, Utah, about 320 miles south of Salt Lake City. I was told the river fished best in the lower section, west of the town. One of the town's claims to fame is that it's the birthplace of outlaw Butch Cassidy, played by the inimitable Paul Newman in *Butch Cassidy and the Sundance Kid,* one of my favorite movies. I also learned that the town of Beaver won a world-wide contest for the best-tasting drinking water (at least according the highway billboards), so I filled up my containers with pleasure.

One section of the Beaver can be called a tailwater because of the dam that creates Minersville Reservoir. As with most fly-fishing below dams, an angler can catch the largest, healthiest and greatest numbers of fish.

In the case of this river, the tailwater after the dam ran through private property. With guide Shawn Saunders again, I had access to that stretch through an arrangement he had with the landowner. A tailwater without public pressure—this combination spelled success. After not catching any fish on the Sevier, this was just the recipe I needed to catch lots of stocked rainbows, which I did. To be honest, most of the trout I caught were in the 10-inch range, but I did catch a couple hefty 15 to 18-inchers...not too shabby. Cutthroat trout also inhabited the lower section of the Beaver, but I didn't see any.

The property surrounding me had it all—goats, horses, chickens, fields ready to be planted, a huge pole barn, a beautiful log cabin and a kindly gentleman owner. The land had been in the hands of the same family for many generations. They actually owned many miles of the Beaver downstream from their ranch as well, which they opened to the public.

Fishing alone on the second day, I anticipated finding as many fish as I had on the first day with Shawn. Unfortunately, my hopes were not my reality. The stretch of land I intended to fish was privately owned, but Shawn had told me the landowner didn't mind the public fishing on this section of his property. In the back of my mind I wondered about venturing onto private property in the land of ranchers.

I hadn't seen any land in Utah without barbed wire fences that delineated property lines, and this was no exception. In strategic places officials or landowners have built stiles to allow access over the barbed wire. By happenstance, I found one where I climbed up and over, and then walked a distance to a spot where I could slide down the steep, gravel banks to the river.

I entered the river a mile downstream from the dam. The flow was less robust at that point, and the fish less plentiful. I waded upstream hoping to find deeper, more "fishy" water. The hanging branches next to the stream grabbed my line and entangled it several times, even though my rod had been rigged in "travel mode," which meant that the fly was hooked to one of the guides and the line was wrapped tightly under the reel.

I had begun to understand the multitude of factors that must come together to become part of the life on a river.

I anticipated being alone for the day, but when I heard some voices upriver, I thought I might meet some other anglers. As I approached them, I held back momentarily and listened. It didn't take long before I identified the group to be a gaggle of wayward teens, higher than kites and very into the "f" word. This didn't seem like a good group with whom to hook up. I took about three seconds to turn around and go back downstream.

I knew the fishing would be more difficult, especially due to the ongoing drought. As it turned out, the biggest problem was not finding fishing holes but rather navigating through the downed branches and river soil that mimicked quicksand. Many of the rivers in southern Utah have this quicksand-like problem.

I stayed in the middle of the river, stepping on grassy islands and gravel beds. My casts landed in shallow pools mid-river,

because I didn't have a chance near the banks that were hopelessly snarled with brush. I had some lightning hits, lost a couple flies, and had no success with hook ups. Late in the afternoon, feeling some pressure to leave enough time to get back to my car before dark, I spotted one last little waterfall that fed into a fairly deep hole. I attached a little more weight to the line and tied on an egg pattern that imitated the earliest stage in a fish's life. Egg patterns are considered a very effective fly and often are created using small balls of yarn. After a few casts, I noticed a flash of white. There was definitely a fish in there. I couldn't gauge the depth of the hole but decided to try a different strategy by removing the split shot and attaching a "bead-head nymph." The bead on the fly served as a mini-weight, and I thought it might imitate more precisely the depth of the insects in the water column.

I knew I had to present the perfect cast so as not to get tangled. Remarkably, the fly landed just above the waterfall and drifted down to the center of the hole, and then *STRIKE!* I had a fish on! It struggled momentarily, and when I reeled it in, it was a very small, yet feisty 8-inch rainbow with a distinct pink stripe, definitely a survivor. I quickly released it back to its home, eager to call it a day and indulge in some enchiladas and lemonade back at Maria's.

I had begun to understand the multitude of factors that must come together to become part of the life on a river. Don't worry; this didn't go to my head. I'll need another lifetime to learn everything.

Chapter 12

The Fremont, Utah

March 2013

—

Quicksand

—

The Fremont, Utah

Suspense, mystery, challenge and discovery are all a part of a normal day on the river. My week on the Fremont River near Capitol Reef National Park in southern Utah lived up to this. I knew I would be flirting with runoff at this time of year but decided to take my chances and schedule a guide anyway.

The Fremont River is located northwest of Capitol Reef National Park. Fortunately, a friend of my sister's, Dana Landale, lives in nearby Torrey, Utah. Dana splits her time between Park City, Utah, and Torrey, where she looks after ten acres and five horses. Dana is a horsewoman, extreme hiker, graphic artist and excellent cook, to name a few of her extraordinary traits. After completing over 1,000 endurance miles in 2012, Dana and her horse were awarded the American Endurance Ride Conference (AERC) National Featherweight Pioneer Award for the season. The Pioneer Awards are sponsored by Belesemo Arabians and are awarded annually to horse-rider teams who complete all consecutive days of AERC-sanctioned multi-day endurance events. Talk about women following their passion! I had the privilege of parking my camper on her breath-taking ranch, writing inside her beautiful home and solidifying a new friendship.

As it turned out, the nearby Henry Mountains had received a foot of snow the previous week, clouding up the river and making the majority of it unfishable. I also faced incessant wind—the kind of wind that takes your breath away if you face it directly. I couldn't count how many times I had to go running after my baseball cap. None of these weather issues prevented me from scouting the river and learning more about the area.

Once again with river guide Shawn Saunders, I headed toward the Johnson Valley Reservoir to see if there might be some fishing above it. When we reached the reservoir, I

discovered it was nearly dry. Perhaps officials had emptied it to do some structural work. We crossed over a bridge, and I looked down on a dry streambed that should have held water flowing from the reservoir. To my dismay, I found dozens of suffocated fish covered in muck lying in a common grave. Very disturbing.

Above the reservoir, the river curved through some flats. Several anglers, eager to start their fishing season early, had already claimed the promising stretches. We moved on to where the gradient became steeper, and the river flowed more rapidly. We found an opening to the river through the thicket, and I tried a "bow and arrow" cast (kind of like a sling shot). I succeeded in landing my fly just above a pool where I thought I might find a fish. After giving it a fair chance with no takers, we hopped back into the truck and followed the river back down toward Torrey, where Shawn had access to private water at a nearby ranch.

On the way down, we dodged a mob of sheep crossing the road. It appeared as if their shearers had their work ahead of them with their thick woolen fleeces. As we approached the ranch, I saw huge black boulders of volcanic rock that were randomly scattered throughout the property. A backdrop of exposed mountains up to 7,000 feet high told the story of past geological events. It was quite surreal. As expected, the river flowed a deep caramel color, and we knew there was no point in trying to fish it.

We gave up on fishing for the day and drove by Capitol Reef National Park following the river southeast to where it becomes the Dirty Devil River, a tributary of the Colorado River. The river does not hold fish on the east side of Capitol Reef, but it winds through red rock country with cliffs, domes, natural bridges and canyons. I gave myself permission to take a field trip the next day and hang up my waders and boots.

Before parting ways, I received some last minute advice from Shawn. "You really ought to try the Bicknell Bottoms section of the river," he said. (This is a 670-acre wildlife habitat that the Fremont runs through.) "Access can be tricky," he warned, "but there are decent-sized fish, and an abundance of waterfowl." Birder that I am, I decided I would give it a try after my field trip the next day.

I loved the day at Capitol Reef. A park ranger explained to me how the park got its name. The "Capitol" comes from the white domes of the Navajo sandstone along the Fremont River that replicate the look of the domes in our Capitol. The "Reef" depicts the barrier-type rocky cliffs that inhibit travel. The deeply eroded canyons are a palette of colors—arsenic, alloy orange, desert sand, and brownish yellow due to the shale and sandstone. I mostly drove through the park, taking time to stop and shoot lots of photos. I yearned for more time to hike into the canyon recesses, but the park closed at dusk.

The following morning, I awoke to a howling wind on the day I chose to investigate the Bicknell Bottoms. I waited until I could at least open the door of the camper without being forced back inside. By the time I loaded my gear in the Jeep, it was already late morning, but it only took ten minutes to reach my destination. I noticed a spring creek feeding the river and imagined lots of insect hatches in another few weeks. I parked near a fish hatchery and walked up and down the road looking for a stile that would allow me to cross over the barbed wire fencing.

The weather had warmed, and instead of a gusting wind, now a gentle breeze rustled the willows. I spotted a northern harrier and a marsh wren and became aware of a fracas in the distance. A pair of Canada geese, which I had mistaken for eagles, were fighting or mating. Isn't that what most couples do? I flushed a blue heron and listened to the red-winged blackbirds annoyed at me for intruding.

I set up my line with a simple nymph rig, eager to get to the river's edge. I slogged down a bank toward the river still hoping to find a stile. No luck. I figured I could probably struggle through the thickets and negotiate the barbed wire. As I stepped on top of the wobbly wires, I snagged my pants and the line on my rod. In the process, my net had been lodged in the spiny thickets. I should have known better. I performed an array of awkward acrobatics to extricate myself from the barbs. My net would have to wait until I renegotiated the obstacle course. (I did find a stile on the way back.)

I noticed a bend in the river that fed into a promising deep pool. Stealthily, I approached the target, knowing how easily the fish spooked. Casting under some over-hanging banks across the narrow stream, I saw no action. Apparently, the fish had fled.

There was another hole nearby that I could fish only from the opposite side of the river. I worked my way downriver to find a good place to cross. I took my first step into the river. Then, my second step. When attempting my third step, I couldn't lift either foot. In fact, the more I struggled, the more my feet sank. I envisioned old Tarzan episodes where quicksand swallowed up the bad guy or, with the good guy, someone magically appeared to rescue him by tossing out a tree vine at the last minute before he went under. Somewhere in the recesses of my memory, I recalled that the only escape from this situation was to drop to my knees and crawl out. It worked, but it took 10 minutes before I reached the reed-covered sod and collapsed in a muddy heap.

As the sun disappeared behind the Escalante Mountains, so did my hope for catching a fish that day. My stomach growled thinking of dinner back at the ranch. I had one last night in southern Utah before heading back to Denver to restock my camper and fish a local river.

Chapter 13

The Arkansas at Pueblo, Colorado

March 2013

A Glass Half Full

The Arkansas at Pueblo, Colorado

I drove through central eastern Utah until I reached I-70 and headed east. Since I would be home for a few days before heading north to Montana, I decided to fish the Arkansas River in Pueblo, Colorado. The Arkansas (Ark) below Lake Pueblo is the lowest-elevation tailwater in Colorado. This changes the norms on hatches, runoff, and fishing. For the first time in three months, I anticipated fishing in 80-degree weather, even though it was the end of March.

Pueblo is all about restoration—new businesses, new subdivisions, new libraries and a few years back, a full-fledged project to restore a stretch of the Ark to make it a great fishery. I love the quote from the Pueblo Chieftain when the restoration took place. "The state is preparing to rock the Arkansas River again. Think fish, not electric guitars."

My drive from Utah had taken seven hours. Once home, I enjoyed the convenience of a full kitchen and the comfort of a king-sized bed for a few days, but it didn't take long to want to get back on the water again. The hour drive to Pueblo seemed inconsequential, so I packed my gear in preparation for a river fix.

I vacillated between wanting to get a guide and going it alone to save a few pennies. Having struggled financially for years as a single mom, it was in my blood to be frugal. What saved me from continuing that behavior was the realization that "I couldn't take it with me." I'd been saving all my life, and when exactly should the fruit of my labor be exploited? My husband and I joke about bouncing our last check, much to our kids' chagrin.

Fishing with a guide can be expensive, although almost always worthwhile. Depending on where you fish, you can expect to pay anywhere from $275 (half-day) to $550

(full-day) plus tip—depending if you are wading or floating in a boat on the river. Guides have often been fishing since their early youth and have developed a love for the outdoors and a need for independence and freedom. They work 12-hour days without a break for weeks on end, and they must earn a year's wages within eight months. It's satisfying, but they work dawn to dusk, then tie flies, keep boats and vehicles clean (or not), prepare or buy lunches...not an easy lifestyle. After searching the Internet for a guide, I booked one on the first phone call.

Heading south on I-25 from Denver to Pueblo, I recalled a previous gig in southeast Colorado, where I was a sort of guide—for librarians. While employed by the Colorado Library Consortium, I worked as library consultant. Recalling the first meeting with local library directors in La Junta—about an hour east of Pueblo—my eagerness to help was apparent. A bit too enthusiastically, I introduced myself and probably came across as the big city know-it-all. Fortunately, the host director approached me after the meeting, embraced me, and kindly informed me that just because these folks lived in the hinterlands didn't mean they didn't know a thing or two about libraries. I left the meeting humbled but pointed in the right direction. Where did this hubris of mine come from?

Having grown up outside of New York City, I must admit I was immersed in a culture of ersatz superiority. New Yorkers believe there is no better place to live in the world. I learned many times over that this is simply not true. Do I still get charged up and love my visits to NYC? Yes, most definitely, but to have experienced life in so many different locations around the country—urban to rural, East, Central, Mountain and West Coast—has been a real blessing. It's still hard sometimes not to be too self-assured.

It was another Colorado bluebird day as I arrived at a lovely park-like setting where bikes and strollers and rollerblades were being unloaded from vehicles. Surrounded by high desert terrain and rock outcroppings, I was glad to enjoy my first real break from winter weather. I looked for the guide's powder blue truck. His cell phone kept him occupied for quite some time, and this set the stage for the rest of our time together. A chain smoker, he oftentimes stood a distance from me on the bank smoking cigarettes and talking on the phone. The few conversations focused on the big fish in this section of the river, but I came up empty-handed for the first two hours. Instead I watched a congregation of killdeer as they searched for insects in their pause and dart manner of travel.

I am a "glass half-full" person and turned my attention to my guide's positive attributes including the fact that he helped with the restoration of this stream. He spent his days off pulling old appliances and car parts out of the river. Through his fishing club, he assisted in raising the necessary money to pay for the stream revitalization. I may not have received the attention that a guide normally bestows on his clients, but I certainly reaped the benefits of his work by enjoying a nice fishery.

As we walked up river, I saw trout-filled redds (trout spawning grounds) everywhere. The fish were a vivid red color and stayed close to their beds to protect their "fry." Some anglers are tempted to fish them, although it's really not a very kosher thing to do, in my opinion. Fish on redds are known to be exhausted and have little fight left in them after spawning. In my mind, there really wasn't any good in fishing to them, plus it's not mindful of the future health of the fishery. Besides, the red-tailed hawks had their eyes on them.

We eventually found some holes where I caught a variety of fish—browns, rainbows, and even a sucker! Urban fishing is not really my thing, but the restoration of this stream allows anglers from the drought-affected southeast area of Colorado to enjoy fly-fishing.

When I returned home that evening, I studied up on the fascinating process that trout undergo to procreate. From egg to fry to parr to adult, it's quite remarkable that any of these creatures survive. The stats show that only one percent does! My decision to decline casting into these birthing beds sat well with me. As a mother, you never forget the arduous process of carrying and giving birth to a baby, and somehow I could relate, even to a trout, in this regard. It dawned on me how much I had connected with the outdoor world in a short period of time.

Chapter 14

The Yampa, Colorado

April 2013

Off on a Snowmobile

The Yampa, Colorado

The Yampa River is the last wild river in the Colorado basin. It is considered a freestone river, although there are two dams in the upper reaches. A freestone can be defined as "a river born in the mountains, fed by cold water and comprised mostly of stone and rubble." One of the dams, Stagecoach, was built in 1989 in 37 days! It is one of the few dams that has had little impact on a river's natural flow, and it has mitigated nature's fickleness in several ways: by optimizing water temperatures below the dam, providing an 80-acre wetland aquatic habitat refuge and designating acreage to a big game habitat north of the reservoir. Every once in a while, folks get together and do things right.

In preparation for three months away from home, my camper was stocked and ready to go. So we wouldn't forget each other, my husband and I agreed to meet in Idaho to fish the Henry's Fork over Memorial Day weekend. The drive to Steamboat Springs, Colorado, went flawlessly—no snow on the passes, no car problems and lots of good music on my iPod. I had never been to Steamboat, but knew it as a great ski town and fishing destination.

I met guide Rob Burden at the Steamboat FlyFisher shop in the company of several kind and welcoming men. We discussed the best spot to fish that day when Rob turned to me and asked, "Do you want to fish some local holes in town or are you up for some adventure?" Without hesitation, I opted for adventure.

Off we went in Rob's truck to a spot in the Sarvis Creek Wilderness area. The challenge with Sarvis in the winter involved access—the snow prevented us from hiking to our spot. So, we hopped on a snowmobile and made our way to locations otherwise unreachable without snowshoes or cross-country skis. The last time I snowmobiled was 35 years

ago in Michigan's Upper Peninsula! The snow-packed road hugged sandstone outcroppings with overhanging pine and aspen branches. Where there were deep puddles on the trail due to early snowmelt, I hopped off the snowmobile while Rob raced through so as not to get stuck.

We arrived at the intended spot and unloaded the gear. I watched Rob intently, trying to learn his way of rigging a fly line. Rob was in his young twenties, and one of the most accomplished fishermen I had met. When guiding in Alaska, Rob learned a unique way to make egg patterns; he purchased clear beads intended for women's necklaces, painted them the color he wanted with nail polish, and then rolled them in sand to make them look as authentic as possible. He followed the bead with a hook about an inch or so away and added a second fly (copper john). It worked miracles!

We stepped into the river as large snowflakes stuck to our sleeves and the surrounding pines. So moved by the wintry scene, I could only think of poetry. In James Russell Lowell's words, "Every pine and fir and hemlock/ Wore ermine too dear for an earl/ And the poorest twig on the elm tree/ Was ridged inch deep with pearl." I was overwhelmed with delight and no words to express it.

After a few casts upstream with a uniquely rigged rod, I hooked one of the healthiest 18-inch brownies I've ever seen. From then on, they kept getting bigger! We remained in the same location for an hour because I continued to pull in healthy prizes. Some were rainbows and some were browns, all big and beautiful. At one point, I brought in a *mere* 14-incher. I hardly gave it the time of day and flippantly unleashed it. "Looks like you need to do a little growing up!" I joked.

Photo by Rob Burden

We decided to snowmobile closer to the Stagecoach dam and investigate another area known for large trout. I couldn't imagine fish any larger than those I had already caught. We stopped in the right place at the right time—an overcast day, hungry fish and unpressured waters—to catch some of the biggest fish I caught all year. The size of the fish I caught in this second location compared with the largest fish I had ever caught—a 27-inch rainbow on the Fryingpan (see Chapter 5), but who's measuring?

Reluctantly, with snow falling, we headed back to the snowmobile as late afternoon approached. I felt like I had spent the day in a fairy tale. We parted company at the fly shop, and I made a beeline to the Mahogany Ridge Brewery, where they kindly reproduced my *52 Rivers* cocktail. After an excellent meal, and feeling sad that the day had ended, I looked forward to meeting up with fellow librarian, David Willis, in the next few days.

At the last statewide library conference I attended in October 2013, I bid on a silent auction item to fish with David, who

had lived and worked in Steamboat. His passion for fly-fishing matched mine, and so I outbid the highest bidder, just under the bell, and won the guide trip.

David and I fished on another gray, snowy day, hitting some of the hotspots in town. The Yampa runs through downtown Steamboat, and so we met at the 5th Street Bridge hole. It is known to hold some of the stoutest fish in town, but they are wily. I did land a few really nice rainbows, but did not have the prolific day I had with Rob in the wildlife area.

We fished another hugely popular hole known as Charlie's Hole or "C-Hole." Located just behind the Bud Werner Memorial Library, I knew these fish would be even smarter. Both sides of the river had eddies that held lots of big fish. I cast again and again, changing flies—bigger, smaller, colorful, and bland—but they didn't buy the merchandise I offered. We mixed fishing and library talk and had a great day outdoors together. I headed back to my campsite west of town and fished until dusk, but the cold set in quickly, and I returned to the Scamp for an evening of writing.

The day at Sarvis Creek was incomparable. If I fish the rest of my life, I may not find another day that matches that one in overall pleasure, but in the meantime, I'll treasure the memory.

The White River, Colorado

April 2013

—

A Blizzard

—

The White River, Colorado

The White River winds west, then northwest and finally southwest in western Colorado before it empties into the Green River in Utah. Much of it is navigable by boat, at least in the early summer months after spring runoff. Since it was pre-runoff, I would be wading this river. From what I read, the White rivaled any in beauty and fishing.

Finding an open campground in early April presented a challenge. If winter persisted, the proprietors hesitated to turn on the water for fear of freezing pipes, thus keeping them closed. In Meeker, Colorado, where I would fish the White River, only three campgrounds existed, and two of them had not yet opened when I arrived. The third was a vast parking lot that looked like an old drive-in theater minus the screen. The rumor was that it had been constructed to house temporary oil and gas employees in trailers.

No one else occupied the site when I arrived in a snowstorm that meteorologists predicted would hang around for a while. Setting up my camper in the blizzard required endurance. I found it rather eerie on this remote, snow-covered expanse of asphalt. There were dozens of wooden posts with electrical hookups resembling peeping toms leering at me as I struggled to set up my camper. I continuously peeked over my shoulder as I released the stubborn stabilizers, hooked up the electrical cord and turned the half-frozen knobs on my propane tanks. Chilled to the bone, I was relieved to clamber into my camper where I found heat, light and the warmth of a smooth merlot.

Waking up the next morning, I found six inches of snow outside my door. I welcomed the opportunity to hang out in the Scamp to write, edit and maybe even nap. The public bathroom was 30 yards from the trailer, and each trip to it made me glad not to be fishing that day.

On the second full day of the continuing storm, I became restless and admonished myself. "Shouldn't you search out the river?" I questioned. "No, it's okay to take the time to work on photo editing and writing," I retorted. I seesawed back and forth on the appropriate action for the day until my mind wandered back several decades to an experience on a seesaw at an elementary school playground.

I learned some life lessons on the seesaw. Sometimes, when playing on it, my friends and I wanted to see if we could balance so that both our feet didn't touch the ground. Sometimes, we wanted to see if we could crash each other to the ground or leave the other hanging in the air. I remembered that balancing had been the most fun to me.

The seesaw was a metaphor for my restlessness. The obsession with river time needed to be counter-balanced with the other activities I planned for this trip—reading, photographing, researching, writing and meeting people. I seesawed on the second day, but on the third and fourth days, I embraced the other undertakings of this journey while the snowstorm raged around me. After a day of ups and downs, I willingly puttered in the camper and put my fishing on hold.

When I awoke on the fifth day to brilliant sunshine, there was no doubt what the plan would be...fishing. I suited up quickly and headed out to find one of the few public accesses to this mostly private water. Following the road that hugged the river, I noticed "NO TRESPASSING" signs plastered along the fences. Nervous to walk to the river with these intimidating signs all around me, I put aside my fears and reached the stream on a pathway lined by barbed wire. Entering at an area called "Sleepy Cat," I wondered if the title matched some rock formation nearby, like the Snoopy on the Green River.

Finding a gentle riffle that I knew would hold fish, I cast upstream with a double nymph rig and surprised myself by immediately hooking a fish. The pull on my rod was strong and persistent, and I struggled with bringing the fish to the bank. Assuming a trout on the end of my line, I was surprised to discover a "whitey" (mountain white fish). These fish, rather bland looking in my opinion, are a whitish, silvery color, rather slender, with a pointed snout and delicate puckered lips.

The fish kept wiggling out of my hand as I tried to remove the hook with more and more force. The hook had lodged into some soft gristle, and when finally removing the hook, I tore its lip. Up to this point, I had not knowingly hurt or killed any fish, and I didn't want to do that again.

In spite of the research and conversations about whether or not fish feel pain, I cannot help but feel somewhat guilty about fooling these creatures into thinking they are about to get some nourishment and instead finding themselves on the end of a thin line being yanked around the river with a hook in their mouth that could be painful. Perhaps these thoughts will prevent me from becoming a good angler. On the other hand, perhaps this would make me a better steward of the fish and their habitat. I'm going with the latter.

Heading back to the Scamp late in the afternoon, my focus changed from fishing to wildlife photography opportunities. Once underway, I was soon rewarded. Pulling over to the side of the road every 50 yards and scanning the countryside, I discovered a vibrant world around me; there were eagles tearing at prey, a posse of turkeys waddling out of sight, hundreds of grazing elk and deer, a gaggle of wild geese, and a mule! After the persistent snowstorm, the animals were greedily feeding on this first nice day, undistracted by a lone photographer. I shot photos until the sun set behind the mountains, blocking the light.

I loved capturing a fleeting moment in time, looking at it again and again, and finding details that I failed to notice at first. Photography brings me closer to nature at the same time that it lets me share the world as I see it with others.

Chapter 16

The Colorado River, Colorado

April and October 2013

Three in One

The Colorado River, Colorado

Rivers like the Colorado flow for hundreds of miles and are so varied in their structure and appearance that it doesn't do them justice to fish just one small section of them. I can hardly claim to be an expert on this expansive river, but at least I floated a total of 35 miles in three different stretches and two states during the year.

Glenwood Springs (April)

The first stretch of the Colorado I floated was at Lee's Ferry in Arizona (see Chapter 9). The second stretch started at Two Rivers Park in Glenwood Springs, Colorado in mid-April. I floated this section with my friend, Phyllis Pool, who decided to celebrate her 70th birthday in a large raft on the Colorado with deli sandwiches instead of birthday cake. Phyllis and I fished together in February on the Uncompahgre (see Chapter 8), which is where we first met. Weather in the Rocky Mountains in April is fickle, but we enjoyed 50 degrees and sunshine—at least during the morning of our float.

The Colorado follows Interstate 70 at this point and the large semis that sped by at 75 mph detracted from the experience as a whole, but not the fishing. The river was murky, something quite common at this time of year, but our guide assured us that we would still catch fish, and his words rang true. The river is almost impossible to wade in this section because the banks drop precipitously and the current is so powerful. We wetted our boots only stepping into the raft and appreciated the guide rowing us ten miles while we cast from our seats.

I usually sit in the front of the boat, but for this trip I settled in the back. I actually liked the new perspective and the fact that I didn't have someone watching my mistakes all day long. We prepared to battle with some strong fish—made so by working out in their version of a gym...the powerful Colorado River.

Phyllis connected with a fish in the first five minutes. I expected it to be as bland-looking as its murky environment, but the vivid spawning colors and patterns on the rainbow were exquisite. When I finally hooked my first fish, I was certain that it was a 20-inch *hawg* because it fought unremittingly. When I finally reeled it in, I was surprised to find a 14-inch rainbow—significantly smaller than I expected, but obviously very fit.

The weather changed in the afternoon from sunny to cloudy, rainy and very windy—not surprising in the Rockies. The wind gusted 20 to 25 mph and casting became more and more difficult. There was something primal about enduring the elements—and I loved every minute of it. Celebrating my birthday on a float trip every year seems like a great idea.

State Bridge (October)

Fast-forward six months to October. I arranged for my husband and me to float another section of the Colorado north of Wolcott, Colorado, starting at State Bridge, a historic site and now a famous music venue. We would take out at Dotsero, a mountain town about 15 miles north of the I-70 corridor. The water flowed at around 700 cfs throughout this section and was slightly opaque due to a rainstorm the previous night. The clouds hadn't lifted and the wind was up, so I knew it was going to be challenging to keep warm and dry. Touches of color still appeared along the banks, but most of the trees had already dropped their leaves.

We met up with our guide, Paul Killino, from Colorado River Outfitters, with whom I had previously fished the Eagle River. Paul loves this section of the river and plans on building a home nearby. A fellow New Jerseyan, he averred that he had finally found his favorite spot on earth and wanted to stay here for the rest of his life. Don't you wonder about the idea of "sense of place?" What makes people love one spot over another? Why a preference for country living vs. city living? For me, I love both—the wildness of national parks to the craziness of New York City—sometimes, it makes me feel a little schizoid. I find it uncanny that we connect to places with such passion yet not really understand why.

At the put-in, the wind was relentless, and when we started ducking each other's flies, we realized that casting was futile, especially with a triple nymph rig. We waited a half hour and tried again with the combination of a hare's ear, a midge pattern and a mayfly micro nymph—but the fishing was slow. After an hour of inactivity on nymphs, we switched to streamers.

Streamers and I had not yet gelled...as mentioned before. They are the fly-fishing equivalent of conventional lures and they imitate minnows, leeches and the like. Anglers must move them constantly under the water to imitate bait fish. I found a few fish using a black woolly bugger, but my husband kept reeling in one after the other.

Now, I have to admit I have a bit of a competitive side, and this really grinded me. Heck, my position at the front of the boat meant I was supposed to catch more fish, and I kept coming up empty-handed. Several of the guides with whom I fished said that using streamers is their favorite way to fish—it makes them feel more "connected" during the hunt for the fish. The moving streamer often elicits a stronger, more violent reaction from the fish, creating a real power struggle between predator and prey. It wasn't until July that I had any real success with streamers, and that was minimal at best.

Paul had been hopeful that we would see a baetis hatch (a small mayfly) sometime that day, which would mean dry-fly fishing. The conditions would have to be perfect: some sun to warm the water and clouds to initiate a hatch and hide us anglers. With rain and wind most of the morning, we were not hopeful.

If I learned anything during this year, it was that serendipity could strike at any moment. And so, right around 1 p.m., the sun came out—not brilliantly—just enough to warm the water, and by 2 p.m. we had a baetis hatch that was prolific. The top of the water was covered with insects that resembled miniature sailboats, and we witnessed a feeding frenzy. We cast dry flies (parachute adams) that mimicked the hatch and watched one fish after another take the flies. It remains one of the most exciting moments in my fly-fishing experience. As quickly as the hatch started, it ended, and we looked at each other in disbelief of nature's glories.

Eventually the clouds rolled in and deposited light rain as we floated through mellow rapids and marveled at the shale and limestone rocks, sediment from a dead lake eons ago. I couldn't help but be awed by the vastness and vigor of this great western landscape. As hard as I try, I cannot put into words what "cannot be expressed." Sounds like something the great nature writer, Peter Matthiessen, would say.

The North Platte, Wyoming

April 2013

Fishing with the Guys

The North Platte, Wyoming

The topography of Wyoming appeared adversarial because it was so harsh and rugged, but I found it inspiring as I thought about its infinite knowledge and ability to link man to the past. There is a wealth of fossils in the limestone and mudstone formations left from three ancient lakes that existed over 50 million years ago.

This is a land where the wind blows incessantly and the relatively few trees live in a constant state of sideways. The spectral light can be spooky as you look out over miles of undeveloped landscapes. Tumbleweed races across the highway scaring you to slow down from 80 mph to 70. There are some beautiful rivers but not many people and roads between them.

I arrived in Alcova, Wyoming, with a topped-off cooler and plenty of wind-resistant clothes, prepared for the worst. Surprised to find a vivid, blue sky and a calming zephyr, I joined up with a crew from the High Plains Drifters (HPD), my local International Federation of Fly Fishers Denver Chapter, to fish the North Platte River. I remembered the first meeting with this group where I was the only woman among 75 or so men—a little different from the norm as a librarian, where women make up 83 percent of the profession!

Unexpectedly, my husband joined me on this trip, and we decided to explore some river stretches without the assistance of a guide. We pulled out our Wyoming guidebooks and agreed we'd stay away from the famous Grey's Reef section of the river below the Grey Reef dam, just a short walk down the road—at least on our first day. This section of the North Platte is always occupied by dozens of anglers. When I walked over the bridge just above these waters, I saw why—there was an outside version of an aquarium below. The rainbow trout were spawning and their beds, called redds,

speckled the river, as far as I could see. I was bold with one fisherman and yelled down, "You're fishing on the redds!" He totally ignored me. There are no rules governing the ethics of fishing redds, but I think there should be.

From Alcova, our first day's destination was about a 30-minute drive to Fremont Canyon below the Pathfinder Reservoir. The canyon walls were steep below the dam, but eventually the river flowed into a large pool followed by a gentle but shallow stream. We ambled streamside and soon found promising looking riffles where we cast our 5-weight rods, that were set up with rock worms and San Juan worms. After working the stretch for several hours without results, we left to scope out new waters. A mere quarter mile downstream a mass of anglers congregated. What had we missed? The story would unfold later that evening.

When we returned to our cabin that evening, there was a buzz about the great fishing at Fremont Canyon. Huh? The same Fremont Canyon where we'd been? Were these fish

stories? Come to find out, some restructuring work had been done about ¼ mile below where we had been, and the fish seemed to have all taken shelter behind the large boulders that were placed there. We decided to give it another try the next day.

Curious to try the storied waters within eyesight of our first day, we parked above the first vehicle bridge below the dam and approached the holes around the large boulders. I went with a double nymph rig and used a Wal-Mart special fly that looked something like a zebra midge but fatter with thicker stripes. It was magical—one after another went for the "blue light special" and they were good-sized browns and rainbows.

On the third day, we joined some guys from our group and ventured to the "Miracle Mile," a section just below the first tailwater on the North Platte—not to be confused with Colorado's Miracle Mile on the South Platte. The wind had picked up on the river, but the sun shone brilliantly. We rigged our rods with a classic nymph rig—an indicator and two midge larva imitations. Few fish rose to the occasion, but there was another rather frightening event.

I had just released a rainbow from a small run when I looked downstream to see one of the men floating helplessly down the middle of the river. Several in the group immediately scrambled to rescue him, as the 45-degree water had likely seeped into his waders, pulling him underwater and putting him in a precarious position. The rescuers dragged him out of the water, up to the shore, stripped and redressed him as soon as possible with only the loss of a rod...not sure "only" is the right word here, since a fly rod might run upwards of $800! Although I wouldn't say that fishing is

dangerous, the power of water is quite remarkable and the river bottoms can be slick and/or muddy, creating potentially hazardous situations.

We stopped for gas on the way home, and since I sat on the side of the car where the gas tank was located, I pumped the gas. A nearby gentleman stared at me as if I had revealing cleavage or a zipper undone. I finally looked at him and said hello. At that point he apologized for staring and remarked that his wife would never pump gas if he were in the car. Okay.... He was visiting his son, Derek Hutton, a guide on the section of the river below Grey Reef Dam—the section that was supposed to be so prolific. Our discussion convinced us we should fish with Derek, and he changed his schedule so he could float us on the Grey's Reef section the next day.

Derek already had his boat in at the ramp when we arrived on an overcast and slightly windy day. His rowing skills were phenomenal. Whenever he found a productive run, he would row us back upriver and through it several times until the fishing stopped producing. The various holes along the drift had great names—Junkyard Hole, Outhouse Hole, Teddy Bear Hole and Bonus Hole. We were most successful in the Wind Island Hole where we experienced a blue wing olive hatch. Derek tied an RS2 with a glass bead on our lines, which helped to make the fly more visible and irresistible to the fish. He swore by this fly on the North Platte.

Here was another of the many times throughout the year that serendipity struck—meeting one of the best guides ever at a gas station, floating the famous stretch of water, catching dozens of fish and experiencing great weather. Life should be so good for everyone.

The Bighorn, Montana

May 2013

—

A Second Home

—

The Bighorn, Montana

One way to bring meaning to life is to find a place where we belong and where things seem to make sense. That happened to me in south central Montana on the Bighorn River where I learned how to fly-fish in 2009. It was not the first time that I connected with life in the Rocky Mountains.

As a young girl of ten, my aunt and uncle booked a vacation at a dude ranch near Creede, Colorado, and flew me out from New Jersey to join them. At the ranch I experienced my first 25-mile horseback ride, fed friendly deer near our cabin and smelled wildflowers that dotted the property. Since that trip, the Rocky Mountains became my lifelong addiction.

Colorado is my home, but Montana makes me salivate! The angling opportunities are boundless, and even though I spent a total of seven weeks in Montana on my journey, I barely scratched the surface of available rivers to fish.

Fishing on the Bighorn is almost always satisfying. Even as a beginner back in 2009, I caught a half-dozen vibrant and robust fish. Unlike the Colorado River that parallels the I-70 freeway, the Missouri River next to I-15 or the Provo River along Highway 40, the Bighorn is far from any major roads. On this river, you are removed from civilization.

The Bighorn is divided into three main sections below the Yellowtail Dam. The first section of the river attracts a lot of angler traffic. Many boats and anglers share this stretch. The second section (from three-mile to 13-mile) has less traffic, fishes really well and is a great choice if you're looking for fewer boaters. However, if you are interested in more of a wilderness experience, the third section from 13-mile to Two Leggins is my preference. Here you can connect with the greater outdoors—catch fish, identify wildflowers, pick mushrooms, watch the wake of a mink, listen to bird calls, observe geese and goslings, be mindful of eagles flying overhead and concentrate on the sounds of the river—gushing or trickling.

Four years ago, I met Mike Kelly on the Bighorn. Mike had just returned to the river to recommence his guiding life after several years at Targhee Ski Resort. His father had owned the lodge where we stayed and so, in a sense, Mike returned to his roots. Mike was a great mentor and intuitively understood my desire to be more solitary on the river steering me to the third section.

Fast-forward four years and several other trips to the Bighorn. I entered Cottonwood Camp RV Park at 11:00 p.m. in a rainstorm in mid-May. Out west, you are always grateful for rain, and so I happily found my camper spot, crawled into my sleeping bag and left the chore of setting up camp for the next morning.

I had a trip scheduled later in the week with Mike, but on my first day I fished with Bob Krumm, a well-known angler, guide, author and friend of friends. Bob authored several books on berries including the *Rocky Mountain Berry Book*. Before we climbed into his drift boat for the day, we took a little hike riverside and examined the black currant bushes and hunted for asparagus. To my delight, we found a couple dozen stalks that we broke off and stashed for later.

Bob had tied on a double nymph rig with a couple split shot and a colorful indicator. He rowed and coached me at the same time, and despite sloppy casts, I caught a dozen 15 to 20-inch fish before lunch—both browns and rainbows.

Lunch was remarkable—freshly picked asparagus, gently boiled, as well as a smorgasbord of meats, cheeses, salad fixings, gorp, desserts and fruits. The portable table and chairs provided the ultimate decadence. Honestly, the asparagus tasted as sweet as candy; I could have eaten dozens of stalks with just a tad of salt and pepper.

We searched the entire day for opportunities to use dry flies, but the first telltale signs of fish surfacing to eat didn't occur until 6 p.m. Generally, you start with a guide at 7:30 a.m. and fish with him or her for eight hours. Not Bob! He geared up for an evening with dry flies.

On the outside of a bend following a rapid riffle, we noticed some hiccups in the water. Fish were rising! Tying on a small size 16 black fore and aft fly on my line Bob said, "Don't worry, they'll have no problem seeing this little guy on the river." Minutes turned into hours and before we knew it the sun was behind the Bighorn Mountains, and we had netted a dozen fish. I started to understand all the hoopla around fishing with dries. It's like a puzzle—understanding the insects on the river, the kind of rise, where to cast the fly and how to set the hook.

Bob rowed us to the boat ramp around 9 p.m., where he trailered the boat and we returned to the campground. It was a splendid day with a seasoned guide. Bob later wrote about our day in his fishing column in the *Billings Gazette*.

I had one nice day in between all the rain when I walked the river and took photographs and met some new friends including Dorothy Zinky, an octogenarian who spends six months in Fort Smith fishing, picking asparagus, tying flies and just enjoying life.

On the next day, I arose early to get ready for a float with Mike. Almost immediately it started to dump rain. Looking

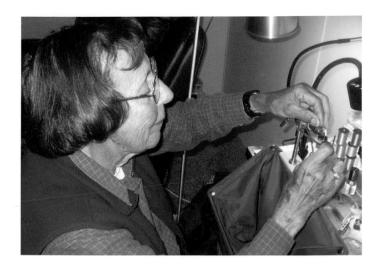

out over the river, all I saw was a monotonous gray that left the water and sky indistinguishable. The birds hunkered down in a wind that blew sideways. I wrapped up in waterproof gear—or what I thought was such—and waited for Mike. Upon arrival, he asked me whether I really wanted to fish. "Most certainly!" I replied. I'm not sure he really wanted to go out on the river that day, but he would never have said no.

Heading to the mid-section of the river—instead of my favored third—made sense in those weather conditions. We started out nymphing, but the fish had hunkered down. That is not to say I didn't catch fish, just not the numbers that you normally associate with the Bighorn.

I'm always curious about how guides organize all their gear and manage the fishing lines. In particular, I like to see the knots they use. One of the most important steps in tying a knot is to lubricate it with your saliva to avoid friction when cinching it down, thus weakening the line. As I watched Mike tying the clinch knot I noticed he didn't add any saliva. I looked up and said, "Mike, don't you moisten the line?" He gave a look of surprise and said, "Shelley, it's pouring raining!" *Oh yeah.*

After six hours, I was soaked to the bone and turned to Mike and said, "I give. Please row me ashore." I didn't want to leave the river, but my body had begun to shut down from the cold, and I couldn't get my hands warm, which ultimately dampened the adventure.

I stayed in Fort Smith for another couple days, but it never stopped raining. No matter, one of these days I'll join you, Dorothy, Bob and Mike, for a summer on the Bighorn.

The Missouri, Montana

May 2013

The Big Mo

The Missouri, Montana

I first visited the Missouri River near Bozeman, Montana, in December 2012, when I took a scouting trip prior to my journey. I hired a scholar to educate me on the Lewis and Clark expedition and the regional rivers. While standing at the confluence of the Missouri, Jefferson and Madison Rivers, I listened to stories about Lewis and Clark and their travels through the region.

I had been reluctant to leave the beautiful Bighorn, but it was time to move on. After a week of rain, the weather cleared and the dry pavement and blue skies were a welcome sight. Low clouds raced across the sky and the grass was sprinkled with dandelions.

For this river trip, I needed to travel 2½ hours north of Bozeman to Craig, where I would search out an outfitter called Headhunters and one of its owners, Mark Raisler. Driving alone has its benefits—the freedom to daydream, your choice of music, the speed you want to go. I fantasized about buying land in Montana, where life is simpler and I would be a step closer to becoming a full-time angler.

Suddenly, snapped out of my thoughts, I became aware of a horn blasting behind me with someone's hand sticking out of his sunroof frantically pointing to the side of the road. My first thought was a flat tire. As I steered over to the shoulder, the truck paralleled my Jeep, and I noticed a drift boat in tow. Lo and behold! It was my new friend from the Bighorn, Bob Lay, signaling me to pull over. Bob was driving home from Fort Smith to Helena, Montana, and he had noticed my unmistakable camper and wanted to take me out for lunch. We exited the highway and shared some sliders and other local delicacies at a highway café and talked of our experiences on the Bighorn. Lunch provided a much nicer experience than a flat tire.

Entering the town of Craig, population 43, I was surprised to see three fly-fishing shops. That told me something about the town. I found the Headhunters fly shop, and they kindly allowed me to park my camper behind their building.

Mark's boat pulling in to the parking lot was my wake-up call the next morning. We chatted about our day ahead, put his boat in the water near Craig and planned for some wet and dry fishing. Mark was a great guide—he understood the river and knew how to teach. Our day together was a mixture of sun and clouds and our fishing style varied accordingly. We started with a nymph rig and immediately took the skunk off with a gorgeous rainbow. The setting was beautiful with soft hills that embraced the river. The sky loomed large with picturesque clouds. Mark warned me that the Missouri had fish that were "fat and sassy." The biomass on the river is so plentiful that the fish have an endless supply of food and lots of room to roam. We caught fish all morning on nymphs, but I yearned to fish with dries.

...and the drift had to be perfect, with absolutely no drag.

Toward mid-day, Mark spotted some rising fish near the bank next to a mellow riffle. He anchored close enough to the bank that I could cast just above where the fish were slurping. Here we go again. My cast had to be perfect, landing just a few feet above the rising trout, and the drift had to be perfect, with absolutely no drag. After you figure that out, your timing has to be right on when setting the hook—too slow and the fish will spit it out; too fast and you'll pull it right out of its mouth. Although I previously had an evening of successful dry-fly fishing with Bob Krumm on the Bighorn while wading in the river, here I was now sitting in a drift boat and could not get my cast where I wanted it and when I did, my timing was off on the hook set. I didn't catch a fish on a dry. *Grrr...*

One of the famous markers along the river is Eagle Rock. From this rock Meriwether Lewis scouted the surrounding area and made decisions about where to next proceed. Although I didn't climb the rock, I imagined a view 200 years ago that would have encompassed herds of buffalo and elk and rivers diverted by beaver dams. I felt privileged to have a peek into the past this way and think about the courage of the pioneers who settled the Rocky Mountain West.

We have not been good stewards of these natural resources that provide us with so much, although many organizations work hard to educate the public at large and our legislators.

When I decided to float the Missouri a second day, Jared Edens was recommended as the guide. In the shop, the daughter of one of the owners cried with joy, "Oh, the Wizard!" I think she got it just right! Not only did Jared look like a wizard, he was a wizard. His kind personality, incredible rowing skills and ability to put me onto fish were nothing less than spectacular. One of the most fascinating stories Jared told me was about his young life on an avocado farm in Orange County, California. He and a buddy used to hunt rattlesnakes for their rattles, which he toted around in a muslin sack. That's a bit of a stretch for "Go out and play, sonny."

Jared rowed me past some eagles' nests. Because of the resurgence of this majestic bird, spotting them is not uncommon, especially in Montana where they are residents. I saw dozens of eagles on my journey but never once did I feel complacent about it. They are magnificent creatures. Unfortunately, man's necessities can be treacherous to them as we witnessed when an eagle was killed flying into an electrical wire.

The Missouri was one of the best trout fisheries I visited. This area of Montana inspired me to pick up *Undaunted Courage* by Stephen Ambrose and delve further into the Lewis and Clark expedition. Something about exploration totally grabs me. When people ask me what I would have liked to be, I now say "an explorer!" I'm no Pocahontas, but she is one of my role models.

The Henry's Fork, Idaho

May 2013

Oh Those Salmonflies

The Henry's Fork, Idaho

The Henry's Fork is known as one of the top-ten trout-fishing streams in the country and the most difficult dry-fly water in the world. The most famous section is the Harriman Ranch or the "railroad section." This 8.1-mile stretch of water has inspired many books.

When I first heard the name Harriman Ranch, E. H. Harriman, chairman of the Union Pacific Railroad, came to mind. He was made famous to me in the movie *Butch Cassidy and the Sundance Kid* when a clerk of Mr. Harriman's, Charles Woodcock, refuses to open a door for the gang saying that, "Mr. E. H. Harriman himself...gave me this job, and I got to do my best!" It turned out that Mr. Harriman's son, W. Averell Harriman, was the one who deeded the land on the Henry's Fork. I did not fish the Harriman Ranch section of the river, and I'm glad I didn't. It would have been equivalent to asking a 5th grader to take a senior math class.

My husband joined me to float two of three sections of the river that I floated—Cardiac Canyon, the Warm River to Ashton section, and the Box Canyon section below Island Park Dam. By far the most exciting was Cardiac Canyon, for several reasons.

First, our float corresponded with the famous salmonfly (pteronarcys californica) hatch. Every year, anglers attempt to coordinate their fly-fishing excursions with this hatch and are oftentimes thwarted for years before they get it right. These beautiful, benign, ancient-looking insects are up to three inches long, mostly dark brown with an orange-brown abdomen, and an orange band just behind their head. They truly look prehistoric. Once the nymphs crawl out of the water and hatch, they live for as long as three weeks during which they mate, fly over the water and drop their eggs. We were able to watch all this happen on our float.

Second, this stretch of river was not easily accessible, leaving me feeling completely removed from civilization—more so than most of the places I visited throughout the year. To reach the river we hiked down a steep—and I mean *steep*—trail to the river while our guide, Derek Hutton, followed us with a large cataraft with all our needs for the day. Dragging that boat to the water required enormous strength and coordination. The day after the trip, my muscles were so sore from the hike down that it reminded me of a time in my 40s when I water-skied after a long hiatus, and I could hardly walk the following day. Sadly, this was similar.

Third, the scenery was absolutely magnificent. This section of the river descended through a deep canyon and had three large waterfalls. Above our starting point was Upper Mesa Falls, the largest and most spectacular. Our float started below Lower Mesa Falls, also a very impressive sight. Wildlife was abundant, although I must say that the fishing captured my total attention because it was one of the first times I had the chance to fish all day with dry flies. We did see osprey and eagles, but not the moose and bears that are often part of the scenery.

Cardiac Canyon proved to be a hard act to follow. When I arrived at the Warm River boat ramp the next day for my second float, I had vivid memories of large fish coming to the surface to take our salmon flies, rapids that made the float exciting, and a profound sense of connection to the river and its environs. The Warm River to Ashton float ended up being the antithesis to the float through Cardiac Canyon. This mellow section of the river brought forth many other boaters and was much more wide open and gentle with long runs. Our guide, Leslie Dal Lago, did her best to find us fish, but they didn't cooperate. We figured they were sated from the salmonfly hatch that had passed through several days before. *You can't eat chocolate every day...or can you?*

I returned to Idaho in late August when I fished with Leslie again. Fortunately, Leslie knew the hot spots on a four-mile stretch through the Box Canyon section of the river, behind Island Park Reservoir. One hole that was particularly productive was within sight of the dam. Leslie anchored the boat on the east side of the river and tied a few nymphs on my line with an indicator. Timing is everything as they say, and it was feeding time with the right fly, the right cast and the right set. On one hookup, before bringing it to the net, I couldn't determine what kind of fish was on the line—it was rather dark looking, something I hadn't seen before. Reeling it in closer, I found a spawning, red-colored, smooth-skinned kokanee salmon! Most people were incredulous when I spoke of catching a kokanee on this section of the Henry's Fork. There were Kokanee Salmon in the reservoir above the dam, and the fish could have slipped through the dam either during a water release or...who knows... maybe there's a hidden population below the dam.

One of the ways to be a good steward of our rivers is to avoid hammering the same spot for too long, and so we moved on. The temperature steadily rose into the 90s that day and as lunchtime approached, we grabbed one of the few shady spots on the river. Leslie maneuvered the drift boat to where we could climb out and picnic under a large cottonwood tree that had some downed logs surrounding it. Being outside and on a river always makes me hungry, and so I focused on the food, oblivious to my surroundings. Thanks to Leslie's watchful eye, a large rainbow came into view in the hole just below where we lunched.

By all accounts, this fish was enormous and for good reason: first, it had found a spot next to the bank where a gentle

riffle brought in plenty of food; second, a large downed log made it impossible for an angler to cast a fly into its refuge. This fish had found the perfect haven to grow old. *We should all be so lucky!*

When Leslie suggested we try to catch it, I said, "Shouldn't we just leave this fish alone?" But guilt has no place on a trout stream. We debated the best approach, realizing it would be extremely difficult at best. In the end I succumbed and slithered into the water. Not being a precision caster, I did pretty well to get my fly in at the top of the pool, but mending was impossible—and thus my fishing line landed over the fish spooking it into hiding. I knew leaving it alone was the better option.

This fish will remain in my thoughts for a long time. Secretly, I was glad my hook hadn't stung it. It reminded me of the famous book *My Moby Dick* by William Humphrey. It's a great story about the relationship between an angler and a monster fish in his home waters. If this were my home waters, returning religiously to try and outsmart him would be a regular pastime.

David Hays, a former editor and publisher of the *Island Park Bugle*, a Henry's Fork publication, said this about fly-fishing: "Fly fishing is a unique way to make love with the mountains. It transcends the predator-prey relationship and brings dignity to both the man and the fish." I want to make love with the river at The Harriman Ranch.

Chapter 21

The Weber River, Utah

May 2013

Let's Advertise

The Weber River, Utah

Pointing the camper south from Montana toward Utah, I found myself deluged with either rain or snow, depending upon the elevation. Nevertheless, the scenery was spectacular because the plains had already turned a rich green, in sharp contrast to the thin blanket of snow from the spring storm.

My next destination was the Logan River in northern Utah, but two problems arose simultaneously: the first was the snowstorm, and the second was runoff. During the months of May and June in the Rocky Mountains, the snowmelt in the high mountains turns rivers into fast-moving and muddy waters. My suspicions proved true when I arrived in Logan, Utah—the river was not fishable.

Onward to Park City, Utah, where I stayed with my sister, Susan, and her husband, Jeff, for two weeks. I spent some wild and happy years in Park City in the early 70s when I met my first husband—when you were more "in sex" with someone than "in love." We made a good go of it and had

two sons, but the marriage collapsed after 14 years with lots of lessons learned. Nevertheless, I always love returning to Utah to visit with family and friends that I've known for decades.

Forty years ago, Susan visited me in Park City when I ski-bummed and worked as a cashier at the Park City Ski Resort in exchange for a ski pass. I stayed for four years, but she never left, starting a sign business from her dining room table. She and her husband made it into the best sign business in Park City. (They recently sold it.)

I maneuvered the Scamp up her long, narrow driveway, while Susan examined the vehicles and said, "They're nice, but you need signage." Two days later, she plastered *52 Rivers* signs all over the vehicles. Numerous times throughout the rest of the year, I had random conversations with strangers—in gas stations and rest stops—and spread the word about my journey as a result of that signage. I think the signs will remain a permanent fixture.

After researching alternate rivers in northern Utah to fish, I chose the Weber. The Weber springs up from the beautiful Uinta Mountain range and after 120 miles empties into the Great Salt Lake. The river had not initially attracted my attention because it had issues with low flows due to drought, like many of our rivers in the Rocky Mountains in recent years.

I fished the Weber with two different guides, each for a half day. On the first excursion, Will Westrate, my sister's friend, took me just below Echo Reservoir where the aging dam was going through a $50M facelift in order to meet earthquake safety standards. We headed toward Will's fishing spot by pulling into a Bureau of Land Management campsite area that provided access to the river. The campground host pulled up in his golf cart to see if we had paid our parking fee, and we chatted for a while about his job on the river. I have actually thought about becoming a campground hostess during the summer—living by a river and driving a golf cart...sounds like fun, and it's the closest I'll get to golfing!

We stood right below Echo Dam. There's nothing especially pretty about a dam. It's fascinating in an engineering way, but it doesn't have much scenic appeal. We watched as water surged from the dam, providing ranchers with their irrigation water, making us leery about fishing.

I have not ignored the controversies over dams, but I understand both sides of the debate. On the one hand, dams place a heavy burden on ecosystems, cause safety and health issues, and threaten wildlife. On the other hand, companies like Denver Water are charged with providing water to their citizens and need to have reserves during years of drought. In the end both want to preserve the health of our waters—they just have different priorities. The two viewpoints should contribute to a balanced, practical approach on dam building and deconstruction.

When I worked as a library consultant, I had the occasion to facilitate group discussions when controversies surfaced. I knew the best way to an agreement was to start with proposing *something* groups could agree on. I remember seeing a poignant cartoon in the New Yorker that focused on a pitcher's mound where there was an obvious difference of opinion about a call. One of the referees looked at the sky and said, "Well, can we at least agree that it's a beautiful day!" That is what I want to say about dams and rivers. "Can we at least agree that we have beautiful rivers?"

I stopped focusing on the cement backdrop and instead started to examine the river. There was a deep riffle in the center to which I cast my line, which held a sow bug and midge fly. Whenever I hit the edge of the riffle, it was pure money—a nice fat rainbow. As stockers, they weren't particularly pretty fish, but they gave a good fight—probably accustomed to the challenges of living behind a dam. So much for the maxim that states "you won't find fish in fast water"!

On my second visit to the Weber, I was pleased to have Marianne McKinney, a friend for the last 40 years, come along and play in the river with me and my other fishing guide, Jeremy Allan. Marianne displayed the same passion for fly-fishing as I did when first starting out. At the end of the day, she made a really good observation—as a former athlete of more demanding sports like skiing, biking and hiking, she was pleased to find a sport that allowed her to commune with the outdoors and not tear up backs, knees, hips, or shoulders. Injuries can happen when fishing, but in comparison to other sports, it's a relatively benign sport— just don't take a dunk at the wrong place at the wrong time.

In its prime, the Weber was well known for its wild brown trout, and we did catch a few while there. Of course, the infamous and ostracized mountain white fish was also a staple. Some say a fish is a fish; others think that these critters are not worth catching. For me, I don't mind catching them. I think they're rather cute as their mouths are always puckered up and ready to kiss.

One of my goals this year included finding a new female fishing partner every month. I came close to that goal, but I counted Marianne's enthusiasm for at least two.

Chapter 22

The Strawberry River, Utah

June 2013

An Aphrodisiac

The Strawberry River, Utah

The ancient Romans believed that strawberries relieved symptoms of melancholy, and in France, strawberries were thought to be an aphrodisiac. So whether you are depressed or in need of some sexual stimulation, strawberries are the go-to fruit. At the time I fished the Strawberry River in Utah, I didn't have need for either an anti-depressant or an aphrodisiac, but the river most certainly provided me with a grand experience.

I talked my sister into fly-fishing with me for a day, and I hooked up for the second time with guide Jeremy Allan. Given the strawberries, Jeremy, Susan and I headed south on Highway 40 past Jordanelle Reservoir, Heber City, Strawberry Reservoir and finally Starvation Reservoir. We arrived at the Oasis section of the Strawberry River near the town of Duchesne.

Imagine this: ultra-clear water, not another angler in sight, easy wading, sublime scenery, 80-degree weather and deeply-hued brown trout mostly between 16 and 22 inches.

We reached the river after a short hike through budding trees, piles of downed branches, and sagebrush with the Wasatch Mountains serving as our backdrop. I kept a watchful eye for rattlesnakes, although it was probably too early in the season to worry about that. Scanning the water, there were fish everywhere—upstream, downstream, rising and jumping. I thought back to my first three rivers this year and how difficult it had been to discern fish in the water.

The fact that it seemed so easy now probably had more to do with the clarity of the water than my abilities, but it was just cool to see so many of them.

Even though we eased ourselves into the stream, we spooked the fish. We remained still long enough for them to return as Jeremy set up our lines with a hare's ear and an ugly bug. Within a few casts, I had my first bulky brown of the day. Susan picked up the casting quickly and made a kind of roll cast upstream after every drift until she finally had her turn. I think the residents of Duchesne heard her cries as she pulled in a paunchy brown that measured 24 inches! How do you explain to someone who has never fly-fished that this

bears. That didn't bother me as long as I had company. I have fished alone on wide, open rivers, but not high mountain streams…perhaps one of these days.

Hoping for a green drake hatch, we realized it was a little early in the season for that. No problem, the caddis hatch was abundant, and we had flies to match. We also encountered midge hatches and black flies everywhere. After nymphing most of the winter, I relished the thought of just a single fly, or at most a double dry set-up with no indicator or weights. Although the rig was simpler, the casting certainly presented a challenge. Newly leafed-out branches overhung the river, leaving a very narrow passageway and limited casting room. Jeremy was extremely patient whenever I snagged a branch.

As we looked upstream, the fish jumped up in the air to catch the hatching insects and happily took a stab at my fly. Once again, I had to find that fine balance between setting the hook too quickly and pulling the fly out the trout's mouth, and setting it too slowly and giving the fish time to spit it out. At one point, I had a stimulator as my top fly and a PMD as my second dry fly. My cast caught a log such that the PMD went underwater while the stimulator was in the air as fish jumped to eat it!

We walked upstream making one cast after the other—some successful, some not—climbing over beaver dams, always aware that we were trespassing on bear and mountain lion territory. If we were not stealthy, we would see a dozen or more fish sprint downstream to safety. Although the river had some decent riffles to fish, there were many tranquil pools that required a perfect presentation to avoid spooking the fish.

We found a pool almost aqua in color just below a downed log, thanks to the local beavers. The pool was six feet deep and held dozens of fish. I handed Jeremy my rod because I wanted to capture this moment on video. It didn't take long before he hooked a beautiful brown, which I have replayed over and over again to relive the magic of this river.

In the end, the only wildlife we saw were fish and a solitary merganser, which looked confused to see two tall, oddly dressed animals encroaching on his territory. He kept his ground until the very last minute and then flew away to find another sanctuary. I had found my sanctuary. As Tom Brokaw said, "If fishing is like religion, then fly-fishing is high church." I had a holy day.

was a fish of a lifetime? She caught another fish close to that same size later in the day, and although we missed quite a few, a return to this oasis is certain.

I had set aside just one day on the Strawberry with Jeremy, but my plans quickly changed. Imagine this: ultra-clear water, not another angler in sight, easy wading, sublime scenery, 80-degree weather and deeply-hued brown trout mostly between 16 and 22 inches. With this description, Jeremy spoke of another section of the Strawberry known as the Pinnacles, I couldn't resist the temptation to hire him for another excursion.

That evening I checked out Jeremy's website, discovering that he was not only a talented fishing guide but also a well-known photographer. So many of these great young guides were ingenious about how to make ends meet—and shooting and selling photographs provided one of those means.

Just like chefs who have their secret recipes, anglers have their secret fishing spots, so details will be withheld about exactly where we landed, but I can say that we fished between Soldier and Strawberry reservoir in the Pinnacles area. Most of the fishing guides in Utah know of this spot, but most clients don't want to travel the distance required to get there, especially because the fishing is technical and challenging. "Bring it on!" I said.

There were a dozen or so places to park in close proximity to the river, but we made our way further up the canyon. We threaded our way through the thick willows until I heard the musical trickle of flowing water where we would have miles to fish on our own. Jeremy warned me that the area was well known for its wildlife including mountain lions and

Chapter 23

The Provo River, Utah

June 2013

—

A Little TV

—

The Provo River, Utah

My Utah fishing plans were enhanced by a serendipitous event in Idaho Falls a few weeks back. When I floated Cardiac Canyon on the Henry's Fork (see Chapter 20), I also took care of some paperwork at a local library concerning a mortgage refinance. The woman in charge of the closing had a last-minute emergency and thus another woman stepped in. After greeting each other, we signed the stack of papers and chatted about my fishing trip. She was enthralled and made promises to keep in touch, hopefully to fish together.

Talk about a woman of her word! Within a day she sent an email, thanking us for our business and referring me to a filmmaker friend who had taken on a new project called *American Fly Guide* for the World Fishing Network and needed a "guidee" on the Provo River. I would have driven across the country to participate, but my itinerary called for the Provo at the same time of the filming.

The producer, Carlton Wing, called me a few evenings later and we spoke about fishing, my journey and our lives. He asked me to participate based only on the telephone call. As someone who is not a good judge of character, I found it remarkable that someone could make a judgment that quickly. I mean *I* knew I would do a good job, but how did he know that? I was certainly glad he did.

To prepare for the filming, I fished the river with local guide Will Westrate. During these days, I learned about the well-known bounce-rig. Because the Provo is so slammed with anglers, the fish hang out in deep holes where it's difficult to get your flies down low enough to drift naturally to entice a fish. The bounce-rig made for an interesting cast—more of a lob—and it definitely caught fish. I also found I needed to use my wading staff on its very rocky bed. Pretty to look at, but difficult to navigate! We also passed a siege of sandhill

cranes, several with chicks. These magnificent birds were at least three feet tall with a call that mimicked the French-style "r" rolled in the throat.

The Provo River is at the seat of the Wasatch Mountains near the famous Robert Redford resort, Sundance. Back when I was a ski-bum, Redford used to ski Park City Resort causing pandemonium. As a kind of groupie, I used to follow him around just to have a look at one of the most impressive men alive.

On the morning of the filming, I tried on different base-ball caps wondering about my attire for my TV debut, but there's only so much you can do with waders and base-ball caps. I headed over to Heber Valley in the shadow of Mount Timpanogos, the second highest mountain in Utah's

Wasatch Range. The peaks surrounding the mountain form the profile of a legendary sleeping woman who died from grief after her lover died.

I arrived at the designated meeting point and met guide Ryan Newman, who would be spotlighted in the TV show. Ryan was not only one of the top guides of the year in my judgment; he was also a high school history teacher extraordinaire. We waited for Carlton, a few grips, some friends, and two cameramen! (They later explained to me that two cameramen were needed—one for the landscape shots and one for close-ups.) Since the show had several sponsors, I put on some Patagonia attire—men's waders that swam on me, and a really nice baseball cap, which became my favorite hat to wear the rest of the year.

Photo by Carlton Wing

We walked the Heber Creeper train track down to the river and wondered about an unexpected encounter with a steam locomotive. The history of the railroad dates back to 1899, when the train served pioneers who settled the valley. Since the 1970's the train has served as a tourist attraction.

Ryan steered us into a location where he assured me we would catch fish...and he was right. He talked me through everything so that there would be less room for errors in front of the camera. Within the first few casts I had a beautiful rainbow on my hook. This hole produced both rainbows and browns that had a healthy girth and a length consistently between 15 and 20 inches. There's nothing like a great guide to make you look good.

We moved upriver to another spot after the fish finally caught on to our game. The day started to heat up as the western sun shone brilliantly, and we knew the fish would be trickier to catch. On the positive side, they were used to seeing a lot of action, so at least they wouldn't spook easily. We caught a lot of fish, and gave the videographers such good footage that before lunch Carlton interviewed me about my *52 Rivers* journey to include on the show. How generous! Everything gelled so well that instead of needing to spend the whole day filming our segment, we finished by early afternoon, and they started on their next episode. *But wait! I didn't want this to end*. I invited everyone to join me for a dinner in Park City, which helped to solidify lasting memories for all.

I later discovered that the World Fishing Network (WFN) was only available on the highest premium cable channels, and thus not on my TV! I was eager to view the segment, so Carlton sent me a link to the program on a private YouTube channel so I could watch it. It's hard enough to hear your voice on tape, but to watch yourself in action was interesting at best. That said, I had several dozen people contact me as a result of seeing me on the show, so I had gladly widened my reach about my adventure.

Photo by Susan Packard

Everyone who participated in the filming lived in different locations around the country, and their backgrounds and stories were fascinating. For example, Tyler, one of the cameramen, had recently graduated from college and had studied French (also one of my majors). We spoke French on the side of the river as we ate lunch, thankful to resurrect foreign vocabulary hidden in the recesses of our brains. The fly-fishing world is about so much more than throwing a line into the water to catch a fish. *It's kind of a secret, so don't tell anyone.*

The Smith River, Montana

June 2014

—

My Husband, Hoover

—

The Smith River, Montana

I have a confession to make. I didn't actually fish the Smith River until June 2014, six months after my year of 52 rivers in 2013. Originally, I was scheduled to fish it in September of 2013, but because of a relentless drought, the river was too low to float. I rescheduled the trip thinking my book would be at the printer's before I fished it, but it didn't turn out that way. I squeezed in the trip in time to include it in the book, and I'm really glad to share the experience.

Montana fly-fishing guides talk up this river as one of the best to fish in Montana. It's remote, beautiful and challenging. I ended up making the trip with guides from Joe Sowerby's Montana Flyfishing Connection. No motorized craft are allowed on the Smith, and only nine groups a day can launch boats—so very rarely do you see others on the river. We floated 59 miles in five days from Baker's Bridge near White Sulfur Springs, Montana, to the Eden Bridge takeout (30 miles from Great Falls, Montana).

The Big Belt Mountains to the west and the Little Belt and Castle Mountains to the east provide a backdrop to the river. Spectacular limestone walls form a canyon on the upper river, after which it opens up to rolling hills and meadows before eventually meeting up with the Missouri River near Ulm, Montana, although we ended our trip 60 miles shy of the confluence.

Our group consisted of six boats, four for the fly-fishers and two for all the supplies for five days on the river. We were a motley crew, two doctors from Maine, two father-son teams—one from Alberta, Canada (accountant and former Provincial Fisheries manager) and the other from Indiana and Texas (anthropology professor and HP business executive)—and my husband and I. There were five fishing guides (Kirk, Steve, Jason, Tanner and Colby) and one guy (Cameron) who managed all the supplies. The guides love this trip as much as the clients even though they are on duty 16 hours a day making our experience phenomenal.

To say our group was spoiled is an understatement. Every detail was taken care of so all we had to do was fish, sleep and eat! Two guides took the supply boats ahead of us and set up camp every night. Camp consisted of a tent for each couple with cots and air mattresses, a strategically located latrine with the prettiest view in the campsite, a dining table and chairs, and a kitchen/sleeping tent for all the guides. We expanded our waistlines with three delicious meals a day highlighted by breads and shortcakes cooked in a Dutch oven.

We covered an average of 12 miles a day. We had to adjust our casting techniques on this river because runoff had not yet subsided, and the fish hung out right at the edge of the limestone walls. If the cast landed four or five inches from the wall, the chances of finding a fish dropped precipitously.

If, however, you could sidearm your cast under the ledges and bounce it off the walls such that it would drop within an inch of the wall and drift along the edge, a 15 to 20-inch fish would be the reward. All this was accomplished with dry flies, mostly golden stone flies, so we had to be ready for that sudden flash and grab of the fish in order to hook it. The front of the boat was definitely the most opportune spot for fishing this river, so my husband and I took turns angling from that seat. On one of the days my husband sat up front, he had the best fishing day of his 30 years on rivers catching one large fish after another. He returned to camp that night with the nickname, "Hoover". (The guide said he vacuumed up the fish!)

The previous week on the river had seen non-stop rain. We were fortunate to have only a few thunderstorms and mostly sunny or partly cloudy days. (The fishing always seems to be better on cloudy days.) On the day we fished with Kirk Gammill, one of Joe's long-term guides, a storm followed us all day. Finally in the late afternoon, the storm caught up with us. We quickly slipped into our rain gear and pulled over to the bank as a deluge of rain drenched us. If only I could have had a waterproof camera to record the fury and wonder of the storm! The wind and eventually hail pellets battered our boat and bodies as the sun continued to peak through the distant clouds making a surreal scene. The wind caused the rain to come in sheets, leaving water slicks next to white caps. The storm lasted for 20 minutes before leaving us behind and awestruck. The sun reappeared, offered us a beautiful rainbow, and we recommenced what we went there to do—fish. This was not the first time during my *52 Rivers* journey that I'd been "blown away" by Mother Nature.

The Smith drainage is known for 70 archeological sites where ancient rock art can be found. The second day on the river, our guide pointed out some rock art that we could spot from our boats. We made a short hike to see a life-like painting of a hand among other figures. On the fourth day, we climbed up some Class 3 sections of rock to reach Indian Cave where 97 pictographs have been recorded. Making sense of the art was challenging, but certainly bird tracks, a snake and lots of finger lines were present. It's difficult to date the sites, but in Mavis and John Greer's paper, *Rock Art of the Smith River*, they state, "...rock art was written about in the early historic records of the Northern Plains," indicating that these were left by prehistoric tribes.

On the third day, we stopped at "Heaven on Earth," an aptly-named destination vacation ranch that also serves as a way station for rafters to pick up supplies, take showers and even play nine holes of golf. I thought I might treat myself to a shower, but they had a group booked for a few days and the showers were off-limits. I would have to make the best of my bucket of boiled water that the guys brought me every night for my sponge bath. Jason, the guide with whom we fished on our last day, told me about the ranch's specialty—ice cream sandwiches made with homemade chocolate chip cookies and stuffed with vanilla ice cream several inches thick. I thought about this ice cream sandwich all morning telling myself that I was already eating 3,000 calories a day and didn't need to devour another 1,000. Of course, when I arrived at the ranch, I saw it as an opportunity I might never have again in my life...and indulged. Besides, it kinda' made up for missing out on a long, hot shower! We humans have such an ability to justify our actions.

The stories and camaraderie that occurred during this trip could be detailed in a book by itself, but I am limited to one chapter. I do have one last story to share, however. On the last night at camp, the guides have a tradition called the "Bacon Bomb." They built up the affair, adding a sense of danger and intrigue, for several days prior to the actual event. I believe it was Jason who kicked off the after-dinner event by placing a soup can of grease, collected during the week, on a platform in the campfire allowing it to heat up. Then, Cameron appeared and approached the fire with a can of water taped to the end of an oar shaft. Well, we all know oil and water don't mix, and when that water was poured over the grease, we had a surge of fire that climbed 20 feet in the air. It all felt rather silly in the end, but we laughed 'til our bellies hurt and chalked it up as our Smith River remembrance. Boys will be boys after all.

At our pullout, we exchanged contact information, took group photos and left feeling enriched and grateful. It was a trip to remember—the Montana guides know their stuff.

Chapter 25

The Dolores, Colorado

June 2013

Love Those Brookies

The Dolores, Colorado

The high and rugged San Juan Mountains provided unrivalled scenery while fishing the Dolores River in southwest Colorado. Having lived in nearby Durango for several years, I read extensively about the highly mineralized San Juans and the incredible stories of miners and their search for gold in these mountains. The miners came to mind as I searched for my own kind of gold—living, beautiful trout. My stopover for this trip was the mountain home of former Telluride Library Director and friend, Barb Brattin. We enjoyed the evening scenery on an Adirondack bench and talked about libraries, the mountains and fishing.

On the western slope of the San Juans, there are three main tributaries that feed the far-reaching Colorado River including the Dolores, the Gunnison and the San Miguel River (which is also a tributary of the Dolores). Since the San Miguel was within 30 minutes of the Dolores, I made an early morning stop to hunt for fish through some of the most beautiful country in Colorado. I tied on two flies—a stonefly imitation and a bead head flashback pheasant tail—and came

up with a single rainbow after working the water for over an hour. The problem with the San Miguel is that it doesn't have a "catch and release" policy and the consequences are a real shortage of fish, according to a local guide.

> *The miners came to mind as I searched for my own kind of gold— living, beautiful trout.*

"Catch and release" is a topic that draws out the same kind of extreme talk and confrontations as modern politics does. Is the modern fly-fisher a brutal and inhuman creature to catch a fish for the sport of catching it only to release it back in the river? Is it better to keep the fish once it's caught, kill it, fillet it and then stop fishing for the day?

Initially, these were questions that I had not thought about. As I immersed myself more and more into fishing and reading about the sport, I became ambivalent. Just like any issue—health care, immigration and gun control—there are no clear-cut answers. There are pros and cons to any position, but there is usually one direction that makes more sense to more people. I favored releasing a fish back into the water and not killing it, but there is a release process that must be followed: reel in the fish quickly, release it as soon as possible without handling it and, if a photo is necessary, prepare the camera before taking the fish out of the net, so it's out of the water for only a few seconds. I really have to bite my tongue when I see a fish laid out on the banks for a photo op.

Leaving the San Miguel, I discussed next steps with my rather gritty guide, Dave Hill, a fly-fishing fixture in

Telluride for decades. Dave recounted stories of classic clients—like the one who had suffered a heart attack the night before a fishing date, but still showed up to fish the next day with oxygen in his nose and a cigarette in his mouth. When I casually mentioned that I had not yet seen or caught a brook trout, he slammed on the brakes and steered us off in another direction. "Lady, we're going to go catch us a brookie! It'll be a rough ride to the stream, but we gotta do what we gotta do," he insisted. He changed course, heading in the direction of a small feeder stream to the Dolores, where I would have the chance to catch my first brookie. I was excited!

The road required his four-wheel drive vehicle as we dodged rocks and other debris. This was old mining country, famous for providing uranium to Marie Curie and for the atomic bombs—or so the story goes. Isn't it ironic that one of the most beautiful places on earth can be the source for one of the most destructive things ever made?

We stopped at a boarded-up cabin that was still in the family of the original mining claimant. The chimney had been removed because snowmobiles had run into it after the cabin had been completely covered with snow from a normal winter in the San Juans. We were alone except for the gentle stream flowing down a steep hill through a copse of trees.

We quietly approached the stream and spotted a glassy pool that had formed after a large, downed tree branch. I prepared to fish with a dry fly—a size18 elk hair caddis on my 5-weight rod. I didn't yet own a 4-weight rod, although it would have been perfect for this river. I made a good cast to the top of the pool and in a heartbeat, a fish rose to eat the fly, but I missed it. "No! I blew my chance for a brookie!" I blurted out. I tried another cast and the exact

same thing happened—a fish rose to the fly, and I missed setting the hook. "You've got to be kidding me!" I said, totally frustrated.

With that hole spent, we headed upstream to the next pool of water. I made another good cast, and almost in slow motion observed an immediate rise, and again, a blundering miss. (I won't share the word I used then.) After a winter of nymph fishing, I realized I had a whole lot more to learn about other kinds of casting and catching. My mantra became "not too fast, not too slow." *Kinda sexy!*

And then there was that magical moment. That moment when I made the right cast and waited the right amount of time to set my hook to find a tight line. I experienced an indescribable rush from having finally connected with a beautiful, small stream brook trout. The little creature measured only seven inches and had a greenish tinge with a sort of marbled pattern of lighter shades along its back. The belly sported a more reddish color with a smattering of red spots encircled by a bluish ring. I released this beauty without touching it so as to not disturb its protective coating and looked up at Dave feeling like I had just conquered the world.

I don't remember much about the rest of my day after that. We did head down to the upper Dolores where there appeared to be some really good water to catch fish, but we were not able to land a single fish in the main branch of the river. Dave seemed perturbed that this was the case in his hallowed waters, but I remained fixated on my little brookie and went home a happy camper.

Chapter 26

The Rio Grande, Colorado

July 2013

Smoke and Fire

The Rio Grande, Colorado

The Rio Grande begins its journey on the east side of the Continental Divide in the San Juan Mountains in Colorado and travels over 900 miles before reaching the Gulf of Mexico. Floating the Rio Grande River in Colorado was an "iffy" proposition in July. The guides at the Duranglers fly shop, in nearby Durango, Colorado, worried that the drought would leave the water too shallow for boats, but I booked a trip for my husband and me anyway.

We were familiar with the area because we had camped near the confluence of the Rio Grande and Squaw Creek five years ago over the July 4th holiday weekend. As we traveled north on Route 149 towards the river near Creede, Colorado, we noticed clouds of dust rising up sporadically on the horizon. It took only seconds to realize a drunk driver was swerving from one side of the road to the other. As he rounded a corner in front of us, we had a split-second decision to make—hold our ground on the shoulder and risk being hit or drive into the gully and take the chance of rolling the truck and camper.

In that second, the approaching car flipped over and over until it finally skidded to a stop 50 yards in front of us. During that time, the driver was ejected from the car, rose up 25 feet in the air and landed on his head on the macadam in front of us. Gruesome, to say the least. I was too stunned to move, but my husband leaped out of the truck to see if anyone else remained in the car. The man lost his life, but fortunately no one else was in the vehicle. Every time I go to Creede, I relive those hair-raising few minutes. Once again it was time to make that drive, and I wondered what might befall us during this trip—once again, I was caught off guard.

Forest fires are part of the summer scenery in the Rockies, and in July 2013, the West Fork fire threatened areas around Wolf Creek Pass. I carefully monitored the fire, since we had to drive over the pass to reach the rental cabin by the Rio Grande. On the morning we were scheduled to leave, I checked the Colorado Department of Transportation site and read that the pass remained open. Although we found it smoky with reduced visibility, we made it over the pass to the Cottonwood Campground. However, Wolf Creek Pass did close the day after we made our trip.

The cabin (located across the road from the east bank of the Rio Grande) provided pretty standard western-fare accommodations: an exposed light bulb on the bedroom ceiling, an old space heater in the living room, some antler lamps and wildlife prints on the walls. We had an early meeting time for our float the next morning and thus crawled into the lumpy, heavily quilted bed early in the evening.

With the fire not far away, it was difficult to decide where to float—up high, with fewer fish, or down low, where we might run into smoke or worse. Our guide suggested we stay up high, north of the fire, putting the boat in at Wagon Wheel, so named because the Ute Indians waited there to raid passing wagon trains.

With cliffs rising 11,000 feet above the boat ramp, we looked north where the sun was shining brightly although the sky was somewhat hazy. Looking south, however, an opaque sky forewarned us of the afternoon's adventure, but not so much that we wanted to cancel the trip. After checking the river's flow on the Colorado Division of Water Resources website, we launched into very shallow water.

The Rock Garden, a rather bony stretch, proved to be the best fishing spot in the morning, although we still only caught a few rainbows and browns. We missed the salmonfly and green drake hatches, but happily flung caddis imitations and PMDs.

We noticed after stopping for lunch that the smell of smoke was pungent. Looking to the west, the sky had taken on a reddish hue. We had no choice but to continue the float, but we solemnly recognized the smoky change in our surroundings. It would take at least two more hours before we arrived at the boat ramp; we hoped that the fire would remain to the west, but when I took a photo of Florian catching the last fish of the day, I was surprised at the color of the photo.

The smoke became bothersome as we resumed the float. Our neck buffs (handkerchiefs) came in handy, covering up as much of our faces as possible, although I felt stifled and claustrophobic. We couldn't see our flies in the water due to the gray overtones of the smoky haze and our throats felt dry and irritated.

An eerie dusk had fallen, but my watch read only 3 p.m. I hadn't seen any signs of fish since before lunch, so I put aside my rod and watched the rapidly changing world around us. The light changed from a dark red to a flaming reddish-orange with deep gray-blue patches of puffy clouds as the smoke billowed up in the distance. Crazily, I felt more intrigued than fearful, maybe because I lived near the Missionary Ridge fire in Durango in 2002 and had already experienced a forest fire in close proximity.

Our guide rowed hard and fast until we reached the boat ramp at 4 p.m., about an hour early. The smoke hung like a heavy fog as we hitched up the boat and drove back to pick up our car and return to our cabin. The drive was eerie because the

sky was ominously dark and the road was devoid of traffic. When we pulled in, the campground was deserted. A Park Ranger approached our car, informing us that the authorities had ordered a mandatory evacuation. Without receiving further details, we packed up our stuff and headed north—the only direction we could go. Fortunately, the little town of Creede had not been evacuated, and we grabbed the last room at the hotel where we stopped.

The views to the west were quite spectacular. The smoke rose above the mountains creating clouds that appeared like combustion from a rocket taking off into space. At that point, the authorities feared for the town of Creede, but fortunately, the fire took another course, leaving the town safe.

The West Fork fire raged on for another three weeks and burned over 100,000 acres, mostly in the Weminuche Wilderness and Rio Grande National Forest, never reaching any structures. In the last decade, the spruce beetle has killed huge swaths of trees, providing lots of fuel for fires; unfortunately, there are a lot more dead trees to burn.

The next morning we returned to our home in Durango via Engineer Pass, one of the backcountry four-wheel drive roads that would take us through the heart of the San Juan Mountains. It would take a lot longer, but the drive would be worth it—lots of opportunity for great landscape photos. Little did I know that we had set ourselves up for another escapade.

Lake Fork of the Gunnison, Colorado

July 2013

—

Equipment Woes

—

Lake Fork of the Gunnison, Colorado

After spending the night in Creede, Florian and I drove 20 miles over Engineer Pass starting at Lake City, just north of Creede. The scenery was as stunning as we expected, although the condition of the road limited travel to ten miles per hour or slower most of the way. A few sporty turns made for an exciting drive, but we arrived in Durango without a problem. In a few days I would drive back to Lake City to fish the Lake Fork of the Gunnison.

After unpacking the car, my first priority was to write up the Rio Grande trip while it was still top of mind. I searched the house for my computer, but couldn't find it. Returning to the car I searched the cargo hold and under the seats, but nothing. I distinctly remembered packing it on the floor in the backseat. Recalling the last eight hours, I realized how many times I had opened the back door of the car to grab various camera lenses to shoot photos. Suddenly I felt sick to my stomach—had my computer fallen out of the car? Had someone stolen it the few times the car hadn't been locked? Whatever the case, at least all my information had been backed up on an external hard drive prior to my float on the Rio Grande, but I would be without a computer. I couldn't resolve anything that evening, so I distracted myself by going to a movie.

First thing the next morning, I made calls to every authority I could think of starting with the police departments in Creede, Lake City, and Silverton and then the sheriffs in Mineral County, Ouray County and finally the sheriff in Hinsdale County. A rather curt dispatcher answered the phone and when I told her my story, she asked me, "Did you say your name was Walchak?"

"Yes, Shelley Walchak," I replied.

"Well, girl, you are lucky, because some nice gentleman just dropped off your computer after finding it on the ground in the middle of a parking lot at an overlook near Lake City," she said in a rather admonishing tone. My hunch had been correct; the computer had fallen out of the car at an overlook on Slumgullion Pass...unbelievable! I felt fortunate that someone had been so honest and returned it. The incident restored my faith in humanity after years of skepticism. (Eventually, I called the person who returned it, and took him out to dinner at a nice Denver restaurant.)

Later in the week, I drove back to the quaint, but isolated town of Lake City, the only town in the whole of Hinsdale County, to pick up my computer and meet the guide with whom I would fish the Lake Fork of the Gunnison, just a few miles away. Most travelers reach Lake City from the north by way of a precipitous two-lane road that follows the river. The nearest commercial airport is five hours away in Denver, so you must purposely want to visit!

In fact, Lake City is so remote and so cold and snowy in the winter months, it became famous because of Alferd [sic] Packer, a miner who ventured into the mountains in the winter of 1873 to search for gold with a party of miners. Packer returned to Lake City alone in the spring. Later accused of surviving by means of cannibalism, local authorities sentenced him to 40 years in prison. At first Packer denied the accusations; however, he later confessed. The case went to the Colorado Supreme Court, and in the end, he only served a few years behind bars. With all the drama I've experienced in Creede and Lake City, I feel a bit of compassion for Alferd Packer! We wouldn't face any winter weather this trip, but we would be fishing in a remote area albeit with plenty of food to spare!

I hired Paul Killino as our guide after fishing with him on the Eagle River near Vail earlier in the year. Paul truly loves his job, and it shows in everything he does. As a former chef with Marriott in Vail, he provided a lunch that consisted of a smorgasbord of specialty Italian meats, cheeses, pickles, olives, etc.—definitely the fixings of a chef and a caring guide.

I drove to the Upper Lake Fork, upstream from Lake San Cristobal, a natural lake caused by a landslide called the Slumgullion Slide, which dammed the lake over 200 years ago. There are dozens of places to fish on both the lower and upper sections, but in this stretch, we knew we would find solitude among the gentle riffles and deep pools.

Unique to this experience, I had the opportunity to fish on some private property with a mile of river frontage, a fabulous mountain home and an upscale cabin for multiple guides when needed to accommodate large parties. A lot of corporate retreats take place here.

The owner made quite an investment restructuring the stream to create large holes and other safe havens for the fish (that they stocked) to survive. Like a herd of pedigreed cattle, the owners tagged the fish so they could keep track of their stock—it all felt very contrived to me. My initial vision of fishing in wild streams with native fish had already been dispelled, but this seemed to be a little "over the top."

Photo by Paul Killino

The river was relatively shallow—except for the areas where boulders and other structures had been placed to form deep holes. We suited up in waders and fishing boots because the river temperature remains cold this high up in the mountains, even in July. Paul's enthusiasm inspired me as we waded into the middle of the river. Within a few casts I hooked a 23-inch rainbow, with a tag on its fin. Paul knew immediately that the fish had been stocked three years ago. Again, a feeling of deceit embraced me as I released it back into the river. "You've been planted here for my fishing enjoyment!" I said to my catch.

Eager to shoot some photos of the scenery, I brought along three lenses—my wide angle, my 200mm telephoto and my 18-105mm. After dunking my point-and-shoot in the Uncompahgre in February (see Chapter 8), I had been really careful with my newly purchased DSLR camera—even buying a very expensive Patagonia waterproof bag to hold my gear. I buckled the bag around my waist and loaded it up with one lens and my camera; unfortunately, I neglected to zip the bag up tightly. On entering the river, I placed my studded boots on a slippery rock and found myself seated on the river bottom in one of the three-foot holes. Before I knew it, my camera bag and waders took in enough water to do physical damage to the camera and psychological damage to my pride.

The upshot of that carelessness was a subsequent $400 lens repair, a camera in the shop for six weeks (covered by the insurance I had the forethought to purchase) and the need to buy another DSLR to photograph the upcoming rivers until the camera shop repaired the damaged one...*ho, hum.*

A major mishap, but I forced myself to regroup, refocus, and return to the business of fishing. There was no point in ruining the rest of my day. I had no choice except to wet-wade now, so I changed into regular clothes and river shoes. For the rest of the day I fished barelegged in the frigid water as a kind of punishment for my stupid mistake.

Fishing that afternoon became synonymous with gluttony. One large fish after another came up from the stream until it reached the point that if a fish measured less than 20 inches, I treated the catch with disdain. (Memories of the Yampa.) Yet, caught up in the moment, I enjoyed the thrill and challenge of catching and reeling in those large planted fish.

I thoroughly enjoyed the day but realized this was not exactly the kind of fishing that most appeals to me. I prefer a small mountain stream, casting with a dry fly on the surface, wild, unstocked fish, and the challenges of figuring it all out. On the other hand, I can't eschew the hunt for huge fish...and guides don't get any better than Paul.

Black Canyon of the Gunnison
River, Colorado

July 2013

Overnighter

Black Canyon of the Gunnison River, Colorado

I drove the long way along the North Canyon rim of the Gunnison with my husband to reach the Black Canyon Anglers' lodge, where we would stay for a night prior to our three-day river trip down the Black Canyon of the Gunnison. The apex of the canyon lies at 2,000 feet. When visible from the rim, the grandiose Gunnison River carves a canyon through monolithic rock walls.

As I made my turn toward the grounds of the Black Canyon Anglers, I found an almost desert-like landscape untouched by rain. The approach to the lodge offered an expansive view of sand-colored hills, sagebrush and cotton ball-shaped cumulus clouds. Leaving a trail of dust behind me, I entered the grounds, where an orchard of apple, peach and apricot trees bordered the road and gardens of fresh veggies and flowers grew beside the lodge. The cabin reserved for us had a sheltered outdoor patio with large flowering baskets where cocktails and hors d'oeuvres were served before a scrumptious dinner. Wasn't I supposed to be fishing?

The wake-up call came at 5:30 a.m. After an early breakfast, eight of us piled into a van and motored for 30 minutes on a paved back road until we encountered what appeared to be an old, pot-holed horse path. The van jolted us backwards, forwards and sideways until we reached the top of Chukar Trail. We gathered our personal items, stuffed them all in large black dry bags that doubled as backpacks, and hauled our 30+ pounds of gear 1.2 miles down the steep horse trail to the put-in. I was thankful that mules had previously packed in our raft, food and other necessary supplies. For the next three days, the wet bag stored all my personal belongings including sleeping bag, mattress pad, clothing, toiletries and fishing gear. The 35-minute arduous hike passed quickly, although my thighs and calves screamed at me later that evening.

Our fellow rafters for the trip included well-known angler Pat Dorsey and his wife Kim. Our river guide, Angus Drummond, was one of the best oarsmen on the river and a photographer published in numerous fly-fishing magazines. As mentioned in a previous chapter, it's quite common for fishing and photography to be inextricably tied together. How can you not want to record the amazing places where fish live?

Loading personal, camping, fishing and eating supplies for three people onto the raft required expertise and experience; Angus had that all figured out. Once everything had been balanced and tied down, we squeezed in. It didn't seem possible that the raft would float, let alone move forward, but it did. A "groover" (better known as a port-a-potty) that served our party of six for the duration of the trip was, thankfully, loaded onto a different raft! The potty was aptly named when GIs didn't have the luxury of a toilet seat and instead did their business sitting on the bucket, leaving grooves on their behinds!

Angus set up our fly rods with a combination of copper johns, black-bodied caddis and golden stones. Unfortunately, the famous salmonfly hatch had already run its course, but I had been lucky to experience that in Cardiac Canyon on the Henry's Fork in May (see Chapter 20). I immediately threw out some line to start off my three-day fishing marathon, synchronizing my casts and mends with my husband's in the back of the boat, avoiding Angus' oars. Shortly after launching, we faced the first rapids of the trip at Chukar Falls. I had the "privileged" front position in the boat (although this is debatable) and thus enjoyed an early morning spray that helped to cool me off from the earlier hike. Just before the second rapids, I hooked a brown trout that went along for the ride because netting him at that point was not an option—I had to be seated and Angus needed to focus on rowing us safely through the rapids. Fishing continued to be productive all day, and between the scenery and the "catching," the expression "died and gone to heaven" took on a new meaning.

We stopped at the Chasm View campsite for our first night. After pitching our tents, Angus called us over to a table and chairs he set up, where we imbibed our nightly libations and savored some tasty appetizers. We retired early after a satisfying and long day. Sometime after midnight, we heard distant thunder. We had left the tarp off the tent for stargazing, so I contemplated getting up to tie it on. But before I could get out of my sleeping bag, I heard a swoosh—the sound of the tarp landing on top of the tent—Angus had already taken care of it. Really! The lightning and downpour came shortly afterward and lasted all night.

Upon rising the next morning, we discovered wide gullies in the clay soil on either side of our campsite. Mud had seeped into everything left outside the tent, and the river had clouded up—good thing we had camped on high ground! In spite of it, Angus served up a full breakfast, after which we packed up our stuff, cleaned the campsite and climbed into the rain-soaked rafts. We caught a few fish in the morning, but after lunch the river turned totally opaque. Without a doubt, a flash flood in a side canyon had occurred and drastically increased the flow, leaving the river muddy and unfishable. We saw debris fields washed up against the boulders in the river and along the banks—another sign of a violent flash flood.

That afternoon the river offered up nothing—even after switching to streamers, hoping to catch some fish down low. So, I focused on the scenery around me. The Black Canyon received its name due to the darkness caused by its depth, its narrowness and the sheer, steep walls. Surrounding me was Precambrian rock dating back 1.7 billion years. This canyon was a geological wonder! I amused myself by identifying the various trees that flourished on the banks—box elder, cottonwood and chokecherry. And the birds! And lizards! Peregrine falcons nested in the canyon crevices while swifts and swallows and red-tailed hawks soared around us. Again, the hours sped by, and we arrived at our campsite.

During dinner, a brood of mergansers entertained us by performing a water ballet across the river. They dove for sculpins, and after surfacing, they would boast about their catch by skidding across the water, although they were unwilling to share with each other. It was a graceful display of cat and mouse on the river.

On the last day of the float we drifted out of the canyon into the flats and bright sunshine, so I slathered up with sunscreen to prepare for the relentless sun and 90-degree temperatures. Later that day I tried to calculate how many times I cast my line without catching a single fish and figured it had to have been near a thousand times...thank goodness for my successful rotator cuff surgery. Several ensuing flash floods through the Gorge made fishing difficult on the Gunny the rest of the summer.

We arrived at the Gunnison River Pleasure Park boat ramp early since the fishing had ceased. Although I eagerly looked forward to an outdoor shower back at the ranch, I felt emotional about leaving the canyon. It gave me thoughtful moments, an insight into its life and rhythms, soothing sounds and endless entertainment. I would miss it.

The South Platte River at Elevenmile Canyon, Colorado

July 2013

Making a Difference

The South Platte River at Elevenmile Canyon, Colorado

After the Black Canyon River trip, I returned home to take care of some business and to prepare for a 2½-month stay in Idaho and Montana. I also had my annual Colorado Camp for my four granddaughters. We took a side trip to Glenwood Springs where we white-water rafted, zip-lined and went to the adventure park, where we enjoyed spelunking and an alpine ride. While visiting an art fair in town, we stopped at a booth where they were selling flies. A conversation ensued, and the proprietors had heard about my journey the previous week at another art fair. I bought some of their flies, and we exchanged cards. Shortly after returning home, I received an email from them offering to buy my flies for the rest of the year! Many thanks to Brothers Flies USA!

I still had lots of rivers to explore near home and decided to fish one of the other sections of the South Platte—the Elevenmile Canyon section. My husband and a friend, Kate Andreae, who was also our local vet, came along. We headed down Highway 67 from Denver through the burned out areas of the Hayman fire from ten years ago. Naively, I thought that the forests would have somewhat recovered from that devastating fire, but the few rebuilt homes had only a smattering of old tree trunks standing—starkly reminiscent of the former thick pine forests.

We drove through the quaint town of Woodland Park where the idea of the *52 Rivers* project first began to form (see Introduction). Heading west toward Lake George, we turned south to the canyon section of the river, which falls between Lake George and Elevenmile Dam. Although it would make sense that this section provides 11 miles of river, there are actually only 8½ miles of water to fish before the canyon walls disappear, changing the personality of the river.

The landscape reminded me of the more famous Cheesman Canyon on the South Platte that I fished in February with Pat Dorsey (see Chapter 6.) Elevenmile canyon consists of Pikes Peak granite, part of an ancient batholith from a billion years ago according to *Roadside Geology of Colorado* by Halka Chronic. As we turned off the highway and followed the dirt road alongside the river, we found ourselves in the company of humongous moss-covered granite boulders strewn along the banks and in the river.

We travelled up the canyon road, passing six large campsites that overflowed with families. Teenagers snatched up holes where they could swim, carouse, smoke, listen to loud music and laugh a lot. We drove further upriver through a one-lane tunnel blasted out of the rock searching for our own holes for the day, but wondered if the crowds had beat us to the punch.

After covering 8 ½ miles, we arrived at the base of the dam. Every parking space on the way up held multiple vehicles. Thinking we had been distracted by conversation and gorgeous scenery, we turned back downriver to look again. Nope, every parking spot was full. However, retracing our steps back toward the dam, we squeezed into a spot next to three other cars and hoped to find a section of river to ourselves. I had never faced this problem before—I had been fortunate.

The huge boulders and rocky bottom made wading difficult, and I gratefully clutched a wading staff.

Etiquette in the fly-fishing world dictates (rightfully so) that you give another angler plenty of room to fish. We saw some anglers in front of us and upstream, so we hiked in the opposite direction until we found a bend in the river without any anglers. The fishing gods were with us! Side-by-side, Kate and I found a place to wade across the river to fish back into a run that looked promising. The huge boulders and rocky bottom made wading difficult, and I gratefully clutched a wading staff. Kate and I had fished together at the Deckers section of the South Platte during my first week of fishing in January (her first time) so the contrast in weather and conditions was marked.

While Florian headed downstream, I set out to play "ghillie" (olde English for guide). I had a lot of fun playing the role of guide to Kate for the day—changing flies, tying knots, unraveling tangles, helping with casting techniques and pointing out the more likely fish habitat. As a vet, Kate probably knew how to tie a surgeon's knot better than I, but she never let on. She netted a few feisty fish, but mostly, we enjoyed the hot day and cool company.

Helping another angler for a day does not qualify as "guiding," although I thought about that and other future possibilities. Could I guide others in learning about the magical world of fly-fishing? What about being certified as a casting instructor? Would I want to work in a fly shop? Should I further pursue my photography interests? How about writing another book—maybe *52 Rivers Redux?* What a potpourri of ideas and choices...

My decision to fish 52 rivers had been spontaneous and engaging. I realized that future plans would probably happen in the same way. I have reached a point in my life where I try to live in the moment and allow each day to unfold before me. I thought of friends who have lost their lives too soon, without having the opportunity to explore a passion. We are all destined to live for just a short period of time—it's important to take advantage of every moment we have by living in the present and not over-emphasizing the past or the future. I loved reading Michael Brown's book *The Presence Process*, which helped me to take responsibility for the quality of my own experiences.

We stayed in this section of the river for the rest of the day, fearful that another wouldn't be available. Toward mid-afternoon, a summer thunderstorm blew in, keeping us car-bound for 30 minutes. We shared stories about our love for the outdoors, our families and pets. Kate's practice at Urban Vet Care in Denver concentrates on working with animals to maximize the pet's—and thus the owner's—quality of life. I think that's a really noble goal.

One of my goals for this year was to encourage others to follow their passions...and to try fly-fishing. When I first started teaching in an elementary school in the 1980s, I had a mentor who said, "Shelley, just try to make a difference in one person's life every year. I know you can do that. If you make a greater impact, more power to you." At the halfway point in my journey, I could say I had made an impact on several people, and I looked forward to connecting with a lot more before my year ended.

Chapter 30

The Arkansas at Salida, Colorado

July 2013

—

Got it Bad

—

The Arkansas at Salida, Colorado

The "fourteeners" in the Sawatch and Mosquito mountain ranges in Central Colorado used to be famous gold prospecting destinations in the late 1800s. Although the mines were closed a while ago, there is still some recreational gold panning in the "Cache Bar" section of the Arkansas River. (Maybe that should be renamed "Cash Bar?") Metal aside, the real gold in the shadow of these mountains is in the Arkansas River in the form of trout.

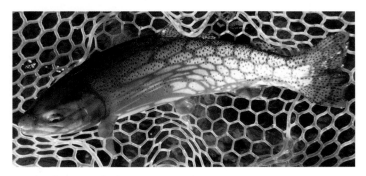

To search for this piscatorial gold, I arranged to float the river with Bill Dvorak, of Dvorak Expeditions. My husband and I headed southwest on Highway 285 through Fairplay towards Buena Vista (locally known as "Byou-knee"). On the way down, we spotted a flock of bighorn sheep wandering alongside the road. Although I've gawked at the majestic Collegiate Mountains dozens of times driving to the Salida valley, I believe it's the most spectacular view in Colorado. The Collegiate range includes Mt. Princeton, Mt. Harvard and Mt. Yale.

My husband and I had not seen much of each other this year, and people often wondered how he felt about my gallivanting around the west. I had a pat answer—"He thinks it's great and wishes he could be with me!" I admitted to him on the way down to the outfitter's shop that this project had kind of taken me over. "I've got it *bad*," I said.

"What do you have bad?" he queried.

"Half the year has passed, and I can't even begin to say I've had my fill. I can't wait to be out on the river every day, and I love exploring the magnificent West and meeting so many new people. I can't imagine going home. When I'm on the river, I feel so at peace. Everything seems connected here—even life and death. The idea of 'living in the moment' frees me of past mistakes and prevents me from worrying about the future." I replied. "Everyone should find that peace in life."

In his always rational way he responded, "Well, you've got another six months. See how you feel in December." (A year after that conversation, I still yearn for the river, but fortunately I've switched gears to other pastimes in my life including writing and photography. However, I foresee another major river trip in the near future.)

Meanwhile, we arrived at Dvorak's Expeditions in Hecla Junction to meet up with Bill, who has been an outfitter on "the Ark" for over 30 years. He also guides clients on the Black Canyon of the Gunnison. As an involved community member, Bill works with sportsmen's groups to protect and preserve public lands for wildlife habitat and recreational purposes. One of the great accomplishments that he spearheaded was getting Brown's Canyon on the Arkansas designated as a National Monument and Wilderness area in 2014. There had been rainstorms high up in the mountains the previous day, so Bill recommended foregoing the upper canyon area of the river (Brown's Canyon) where he thought the river might be too murky. Instead, our launch would be at Rincon, where he thought the river would be clearer and fewer people would be fishing. Brown's Canyon is by far the most famous section of the river in the valley and offers exciting rafting and fishing, but we were content to float this section of the Ark.

Like many rivers I have fished this year, public access is less than ideal on the Ark—only about 40 percent of it is accessible to the public. In Colorado, once a boat is launched from a public boat ramp, you can float it without obstruction as long as you don't put your feet on the river bottom where the land is private. One woman had more "No Trespassing" signs than I've ever seen before. I struggle with our rivers and banks not being accessible to all.

It was a picture-perfect day in Colorado—a slight wind, some low stratus clouds and a moderate temperature. Shortly after launching, we hit the first Class 3 rapids, which offered a gentle, cooling spray. The river was semi-transparent, and we anticipated catching quite a few of the large browns and rainbows for which the river is famous. As our boat drifted downstream, the lava-formed walls of the canyon took on various hues of gold, sand and cobalt blue.

We started fishing with a Royal Wulff and a renegade, but we only picked up a couple fish. After giving the dries a "good go," we succumbed to the underworld of nymphs, using mostly pheasant tails, PMD nymphs and copper johns. Even with the change in flies, the fish only fed sporadically. And so I welcomed the chance to observe the world around me and take photographs. Sometimes I wondered why I focused solely on the 1-inch clear or salmon-colored thingamabobber floating on the current for so many hours when I had amazing scenery surrounding me!

Although I've gawked at the majestic Collegiate Mountains dozens of times driving to the Salida valley, I still believe it's the most spectacular view in Colorado.

We fished hard all day, but the trout never fully cooperated. I found a few nice browns, but not what I expected from the Ark. Bill scratched his head, not understanding why the fish weren't hungry after many days of fast and cloudy water. We certainly hooked several nice fish, but it just wasn't what I had expected from the Arkansas. I wasn't disappointed though. One of the lessons that I've learned is that anglers don't catch fish every day, no matter how great they are... and I was still a beginner.

Chapter 31

South Fork of the Snake, Idaho

August 2013

—

Moms and Sons

—

South Fork of the Snake, Idaho

Understanding how the Rocky Mountain drainages flow can be quite a challenge. After browsing several books and having a multitude of conversations about the Snake River, I finally figured it out. The South Fork of the Snake is fed from Wyoming's Snake River, which originates in the southern region of Yellowstone Park. The Henry's Fork (actually the North Fork of the Snake River) and the South Fork of the Snake join together about 30 miles north of Idaho Falls near Menan Buttes, where the river once again becomes known as the Snake River and flows westward across Idaho. I fished the Henry's Fork through Cardiac Canyon (see Chapter 20) in May and fished another section after Island Park Dam in early August, but this trip was a float down the South Fork of the Snake, hereafter referred to as the South Fork.

I drove to Idaho Falls to meet my son, Michael, who had flown from Detroit for a few days of fishing in Idaho and a short jaunt to the Northwest. I can understand why, in 2010, *Bloomberg Businessweek* designated Idaho Falls as one of the best places to raise kids. As a hub for most of eastern Idaho and western Wyoming, it provides easy access to the great outdoors with a high standard of living. The beautiful Idaho Falls, right in the heart of the city, was impressive and provided much of the electrical needs of the region.

Even though he had been one of the most ardent readers of my *52 Rivers* blog, my "city" son Michael had never fly-fished before. I couldn't believe he was willing to take a week of vacation to fish with his mother. As a sales manager for a men's skin product called Turo, he was a little freaked out about the intensity of the sun, but lathered up with a product he sells and covered his face and neck with a buff.

We met our guide, Trevor Wine, at the boat ramp where we would take off on a 16-mile float that day. Mike took the front seat in the boat, while I climbed into the back. It was uncommon for me to sit in the back of the boat, a ClackaCraft, and I relished it. For most of the year I had been on such a steep learning curve under many guides' watchful eyes; in the rear, I had the opportunity to practice unobserved what I had learned.

The piscatorial madness of the early summer hatches on the South Fork is well known, but we fished the river after the famous hatches—in the hot, lazy days of August. Trevor set me up with a foam golden stone fly and turned his attention to Mike, setting him up with the same, along with a pheasant tail dropper on a jig rig. Trevor rowed within casting distance of the bank, and I did my best to entice the cutthroats, rainbows and browns from the overgrowth without catching my fly on the grasses or branches.

Trevor put into play all his pedagogical skills and made a wannabe angler out of Mike that day, (although a few four-letter words would escape from Mike's mouth before he brought in his first fish). He coached Mike:

"Good spot ten feet up on the right!" Trevor yelled out. Oops, cast too short.

"Try again, under that broken-off branch." Oops, a snag.

"Ok, up ahead on the outside edge of the riffle." This time Mike's cast was right on, and he was awarded a good-sized mountain whitefish. While manning the oars and teaching Mike, Trevor (a multi-tasker, for sure) released a rainbow from my line. The fun had just begun!

The first fish he caught, a whitefish, was not really the prize he was after, but he didn't know that, and enjoyed the tug-fix. We told him that seeing whitefish is a sign of a healthy river, which is assuredly true. He later hooked and released several hefty browns, including one that was 21- inches, the true gift of the day.

Trevor showed me the well-known "South Fork slap" —a rather violent presentation that mimics a large bug falling clumsily and noisily on the surface. It signals a smorgasbord of large protein, (like a porterhouse steak) and the fish strike at it aggressively. Although I didn't use the fly most famous for this action, the Super X, my foam golden stonefly had the same effect, and the technique attracted one fish after another. It wasn't too long before I had a grand slam of a cutthroat, rainbow, brown, and yes, several whiteys.

Focused so keenly on fishing, we were astonished to find it was already mid-afternoon, and we hadn't even thought about food. WorldCast Anglers has quite a posh picnic area that also serves as an overnight stopover for their multiple-day floats. The outhouse was fancied up with wildflowers blooming in front, and once inside, I found the latest issue of *Fly Fisherman* magazine. A nearby canvas tent on floorboards with two twin beds has housed the likes of Dick Cheney (with a fly rod, not a gun). Fly-fishing is about the only thing I have ever had in common with him.

After lunch, we passed by the largest eagle breeding ground in the lower 48 states and were excited to see at least a dozen eagles, ranging from early juveniles to mature adults. The cottonwoods along the banks also harbored 126 bird species including osprey, herons and 21 varieties of raptors.

Moose are commonly seen, although we didn't spot any that day. The high volcanic cliffs and surrounding lodgepole pine forests also provide protection for all kinds of wildlife.

The South Fork is considered a "rowdy" river, which means it can be dangerous to wade except in the fall when the water level drops. We floated the river at 9,700 cfs (cubic feet per second). Trevor has seen the river at 22,000 cfs! I never really understood how to relate that measurement to something that made sense to me, but Trevor provided an excellent analogy. Imagine a basketball, which is about a cubic foot in size. Now imagine 9,700 of them floating past you in the river every second. That gave me a very clear idea of cfs. As with a river, people can also be rowdy, as we witnessed with a boat that had been grounded because the captain couldn't make the turn at the speed he approached the curve. We later found out that the accident actually caused a death....

Late afternoon was upon us before we knew it, and the catching had waned, which is usually the case on the last stretch of the trip. Trevor had planned to motor the last five miles or so, and it was time. Reluctant to leave, I wondered how many moms have had the opportunity to spend a day on a beautiful river with an adult son. I always feel sad when a great angling day comes to a close, but this day I really didn't want to end. At least I had one more day on another Idaho river to share with Mike.

Chapter 32

The Little Wood, Idaho

August 2013

I Love Woolly Buggers

The Little Wood, Idaho

It was a long time coming and it took a lot of work, but I learned to love woolly buggers on the Little Wood River in central Idaho because they finally returned the love. A woolly bugger is a streamer, which demands constant movement in order to mimic the action of a small fish. I fumbled miserably the first time I tried streamers on the Bighorn River several years ago, and I continued to be rather inept with them.

> *It was a long time coming and it took a lot of work, but I learned to love woolly buggers...*

The woolly bugger and I are also connected through fly-tying. It was the first and only fly that I had tied during a class at the Denver Orvis shop before I started my journey. Although I had great plans to tie flies every night throughout the year on the road, I was not able to make that commitment.

The Little Wood is a river in Central Idaho that originates in the Pioneer Mountains. The original plan was to fish the nearby Big Wood River in Idaho, but low water waylaid the plans. Our guide, John Huber, recommended we try the Little Wood. My son, Michael, and I had floated the South Fork of the Snake earlier in the week (see Chapter 31), and I wanted him to experience wading in a river as well. The odds were against us as we approached this river. First, it was also very low—just not as low as the Big Wood—and second, we couldn't make it over to Picabo until the afternoon, so we would be fishing in the heat of the day.

From Idaho Falls, we headed west and passed through the Craters of the Moon National Monument, which is described on its website as "a vast ocean of lava flows with scattered islands of cinder cones and sagebrush." I agreed with their assessment of it being a "weird and scenic landscape" where you can get a modern-day glimpse of the remains of violent eruptions from 15-20,000 years ago.

Once we met John at the Picabo Angler, we drove through a lava rock and sagebrush desert that was bisected by basalt ridges on our way to the Taylor "Bear Tracks" Williams Recreation area. Everything looked desolate except the river banks with thickly-lined green willows—like a painted mirage in the desert. We watched for rattlesnakes on the hike down to the river. I had been warned several times to keep an eye out for them throughout the year but, thankfully, never saw one.

When we reached the river, the landscape changed from high mountain desert to a strip of cottonwoods and willows, and I was surprised at the mere trickle of the stream. There were some undercut bank pools and the occasional shallow riffle, but it didn't look too promising. John knew better. He rigged me up with a parachute adams and sent me upstream to a promising-looking pool so he could work with Michael on some nymph fishing. It wasn't long before I heard a few shouts and was happy to see that Michael had caught a nice rainbow.

Idaho Fish and Game stocks about 4,000 rainbows and 3,000 browns in the Little Wood every year. I'm curious not only about the process of stocking fish, but also wonder what a new occupation of fisheries biologist would be like...*I need another lifetime.*

In the meantime, I cast close to the shaded banks as well as in the deeper pools, but the heat was bearing down, and unlike us, the fish were smart enough to stay away from the sun. They were not going to rise to the surface in the warm, un-oxygenated water.

So, John recommended we try to get to the bottom of the big holes to see if the fish would eat down there; it was worth a try, since I hadn't seen any action up top. It's just that "on the bottom" meant a streamer and my track record with streamers wasn't stellar.

John identified the hole where he wanted me to cast after attaching a standard black woolly bugger, and he stood aside as I let it rip. He instructed me to give it some time to sink, and then start stripping in the line.

Strip, strip, pause.

Strip, pause, strip.

Strip, strip, strip.

"Try it again and slow down a bit," said John. "It's the same process, but strip in shorter lengths." Nothing.

John cheered me on. "OK, try again, but this time speed it up a little."

"John! There's a tug on my line!" I yelled out. Another series of instructions: "Keep the line tight; slowly lift the tip of your rod and keep stripping; don't trip on your line; move a little to the left." And, there it was—a red-slabbed rainbow. What a rush! And so I tried again in another hole

Photo by John Huber

and found another fish. We took lots of photos and even a video of the experience—reassurance that I really did catch a fish on a streamer.

My son memorialized the day for me and had a painting made from one of our photographs. The artist, Joe Rayome, lives in New York City. It has a prominent spot in my home, so I can recall the day on the Little Wood River that I amassed some love from my son and a streamer.

Painting by Joe Rayome

Chapter 33

Middle Fork of the Salmon, Idaho

August 2013

River of No Return

Middle Fork of the Salmon, Idaho

Perhaps my most adventuresome experience of the year involved a flight with pilot Mike Hart to the Middle Fork of the Salmon where we would fish together for the weekend. With the nearby fires, I wondered about flying in a small, two-seater Cessna 180 to the 2.3 million acre Frank Church River of No Return, especially since I'd never flown in a plane smaller than a 737. A backcountry pilot with over 30 years' experience, Mike picked me up at the small grass airstrip in Picabo, Idaho, and off we flew to explore the river.

A smoky haze impeded the view from our plane at 11,000 feet, but as we flew further north, past the Pioneer and White Cloud Mountains, the smoke abated. Just north of these ranges and the Sawtooth Mountains, lay the headwaters of the Middle Fork of the Salmon. We flew over the mountain peaks and looked down on rugged, deep canyons, where we beheld the various drainages. Mike pointed out the slim line of blue water that was the Middle Fork. That river is known as the most prolific westslope cutthroat fishery remaining in North America, and is reachable only by raft, small plane, foot or horseback.

As the plane approached the Indian Creek landing strip, a popular drop-off point for rafters when the upper river is too thin to float, the water drew my focus. It looked like a long piece of aqua-colored ribbon speckled with white spots of rapids. Pine forests decorated the surrounding mountains, and there wasn't a town or any other sign of civilization in sight. In the midst of all this, Mike expertly landed the plane on a dirt strip less than a mile long. The touchdown was so gentle I hardly knew the plane was on the ground. I became a small-plane convert!

We chose a campsite that overlooked the river and the remains of a forest that had been burned by a fire in 2000.

The crown fire hadn't crossed the river, so we were nestled in a grove of ponderosa pines. We stuck our noses in the crevices of the bark and were rewarded with the delightful fragrance of butterscotch. At 10 a.m., we were ready to go on the hunt.

As any seasoned angler knows, August is hopper time. Mike and I set up our 5-weight rods with foam-bodied hoppers and pheasant tail droppers. We hiked a quarter mile downstream, in the opposite direction of the rafting groups, and found a fishy-looking run followed by a deep pool. The river was running low and gin clear.

I cast to the edge of a run and immediately hooked a 10-inch rainbow with my hopper. Mike looked over and gave me a thumbs-up—my head swelled a bit as I began to have confidence in my angling skills. Several casts later, I caught a gorgeous 14-inch westslope cutthroat with the brilliantly distinctive salmon-colored slash on its lower jaw. The pectoral, pelvic and anal fins also had a noticeable white border.

After lunch, we headed down to the confluence of Indian Creek and the Middle Fork to explore, expecting to find some untouched water and hungry fish. In the heat of the day, we persevered along a rather sketchy trail for a mile by the bank of the creek. Dunking our feet in the water helped to cool off our bodies. The streambed was a motley-colored palette of greens, tans, blues, reds and yellows and was incredibly slippery. My rubber-soled wading shoes were not effective, and I'd left behind my wading staff. The stream was shallow and not fast-flowing so I managed fairly well with my wading, but not so well with fishing.

I rigged up with a purple haze dry fly even though we didn't see any rising fish. With no lookers, still hoping to fish with dry flies, I changed back to a hopper. Again, no bites. I added a copper john dropper and ended up with several 6-inch rainbows that fought like monsters. I doubt they'd ever been caught, and I disliked being the first to hook them, so I took off the dropper. Mike caught a few 10-inch fish but we decided to head back to the main river to find another hole on the way back to camp.

We straggled through downed trees until we reached our last haunt of the day. Mike ventured into the river, nearly chest deep, to reach some dry rocks from which to cast. He successfully reeled in several of the river's standard fare—10 to12-inch cutthroats mostly using a hopper/dropper rig. I decided to try a foam attractor whose name I didn't know, but we called it "Marilyn" because it was so sexy looking with its pink midriff and white fuzz. The fish were not in the least bit interested in Marilyn, and we concluded that our rather bland-looking, medium-sized flies had been most successful, at least on this first day of fishing.

Back at camp, we indulged in a nice bottle of wine and a scrumptious dinner of homegrown everything. We crashed at 9:30 p.m. and heard some hearty partying going on in the rafting camp up river. Tempted to join them, I opted instead for some thinking time to revel in my day and strategize for the next.

I awakened to a chilly morning with temps in the 40s and the smell of bacon frying. We shared a pound of bacon then moved on to scrambled eggs, homemade bread, yogurt and granola while telling fishing and life stories—and then we both became antsy to get back on the river.

We hiked upriver and found a perfect spot next to a fast moving riffle. Since success the previous day came with a bland, tan-colored hopper, we started out with the same. Mike landed a nice cutthroat after a few casts. I plugged

away and changed my position several times. Results: me, nothing; Mike, a continuous stream. It turned into a day of line management for me. I changed flies incessantly and even compromised my summer standard by putting on some droppers. Later, I connected with a few 10-inch cutties but that was the best I could do on that day.

We had to rise early the next morning to make sure we were airborne before the air warmed up, so we reluctantly left the river. Dinner back at the camp consisted of homegrown tomatoes, fresh basil, mozzarella and a drizzle of olive oil and balsamic vinegar. With the wine gone, we indulged in a nightcap of some Johnny Walker Green Label Scotch.

The next morning as the sun brightened the day, we waited for five other small planes to land before we took off. For a sense of future trips, Mike landed the plane at a few other landing strips before dropping me back off in Picabo. Each strip was a little more challenging because of shorter runways, doglegs and bumps on the strip.

Once called the "River of No Return," I knew that would certainly not be the case for me.

I was in awe of the complex mixture of rock, water and fish. There were dozens of tributaries and canyons that I am sure housed an abundance of wildlife seeking refuge from the heat. I thought I would see more wildlife in this wilderness area, but our checklist included only a single white-tailed deer, several chipmunks, bats, a handful of garter snakes, an osprey and an abundance of cedar waxwings. Once called the "River of No Return," I knew that would certainly not be the case for me.

Chapter 34

Silver Creek, Idaho

Row vs Wade: The Perfect Solution

Silver Creek, Idaho

At least 25 forest fires were burning in Idaho, scaring away tourists and anglers because of closed roads, impeded views and skies filled with smoke. Fly-fishing can be tricky in the late summer in the Rocky Mountains, but especially so with fires and droughts. The riverbeds had lost depth and the water temperatures warmed up, causing the fish to find shelter in the deepest, non-accessible holes. The hatches were few, and dry-fly fishing became difficult, at best.

Under these conditions, I returned to Picabo, Idaho, to fish Silver Creek, a spring-fed beauty. During the research phase, prior to starting my *52 Rivers* journey, Silver Creek had not caught my attention. When I arrived in Idaho in early August, I heard from many sources that it was a river not to be missed, and so I changed my plans. I was so glad I did.

I met up with John Huber, a 20-year guide on this river, and my guide on the Little Wood (see Chapter 32). Postponing the trip by a week to dodge the smoke and fires, I was lucky that late summer monsoons had occurred, clearing the air.

John told me to put on waders and a warm pair of socks, which surprised me, as I had been wet-wading for the last two months. Really? In 90-degree weather? We were going fishing on a private section of the river that belonged to the Double R Fishing Club. The club was located on a well-known piece of land—the K Bar K Purdy Ranch. Float tubes were the order of the day, putting in below the Nature Conservancy where there was public access to the river.

As we drove to our fishing spot without another soul in sight, John warned me that fly-fishing Silver Creek, like parts of the Henry's Fork, was considered to be graduate-level fly-fishing. "This is not a numbers game," said John. "You will do well to catch a few really nice fish."

We placed our float tubes—or belly boats—at the edge of the water, stepped inside them and surreptitiously made our way into the river at around 7:30 a.m. It became immediately evident why I needed waders and warm socks in the clear, cold, spring-fed stream; we would be in the water for many furtive hours with very little movement. We needed to be there early before the river warmed up, but not too early since the expected trico hatch required sun-warmed water from the previous night's chill.

Golden-hued, lime green reeds decorated the horizon line. Puffy cumulus clouds and the gentle brown Picabo Hills were reflected in the water. The banks on the south side of the river were shadowed, and the stillness in the air and water was broken only by the rises of fish and birdcalls.

We stealthily made our way to the middle of the river with soft voices and as little movement as possible, using only one leg gently placed on the riverbed to propel us forward. John handed me a slow-action 4-weight Winston rod with a hackle stacker fly on the leader. We waited for the hatch. In the meantime, I watched several fish feeding consistently, rippling the water every 20-30 seconds on the surface. On the hunt, we studied the rises and our points of attack. I pictured Ernest Hemingway on Silver Creek—the place he made his mark, and I felt privileged to have the opportunity to follow in his footsteps.

After casting in the middle of the river to judge my casting distance, I aimed my first cast about three feet above a rise that was occurring regularly. I was perched tall in my seat (yes, these tubes have little seats made of netting) as my fly glided right over the center of the water ripples where the fish had been rising. Nothing. I cast again. "Come on, EAT IT," whispered John. I finished the drift...cast again...oops, bad cast...cast again. "Closer to the bank!" Cast again. "OK, let's move down river a bit." Stealthily, I cast again...and again...and again...with no takers.

About 45 minutes into our time on the river, I made a nice cast into some water near the bank on the south side of the river, and I saw the fish rise. Timed perfectly, I lifted the rod tip and felt the familiar tug of the fish. "Keep the tension on the line, but don't fight too hard." Within a few breath-taking minutes, I beheld my first Silver Creek rainbow. It wasn't a large fish, but its colors were rich and bold. The fish were not going to come easily here.

The trico hatch never happened that day; in fact, we didn't see any hatches. I had the opportunity at several other fish but either they spit out the fly or my timing was off. I didn't land another fish that morning. No matter, we floated down the river until our stomachs called for food back at the Picabo Angler fly shop and community hangout.

During lunch, I met some of the locals including Nick Purdy, son of the 95-year-old patriarch of the valley, Bud Purdy. His concern for the health and welfare of the land and the people who live there was apparent from the discussions John and I had about the valley. The Nature Conservancy, just north of where we fished, is a shining example of the work being done to preserve the fishery.

We changed fishing locations after lunch and headed to the Purdy ranch on the north side of Highway 20. Cattle huddled around watering holes as we made our way through barbed wire gates to a river that seemed totally pristine. I hoped to see another fish or two that afternoon, casting with hoppers.

Once again, we strode into the water with float tubes and the Winston 4-weight in tow, but this time we tied on some "real hoppers" or "chicken hoppers" on my line. I loved the slow-action 4-weight rod that seemed to better fit my

natural rhythm of casting. It was nice to get to the point where I could tell the difference. The famous angler Joan Wulff used a Winston rod, so I had big wading shoes to fill.

The bottom of the river was filled with aquatic salad—lots and lots of greens to make our way through. Every movement we made probably created waves or some other warning signal to the easily spooked fish. I can't say I didn't have any opportunities, but they were few and far between. I stayed focused, but the thrill of seeing a fish flashing got the better of me as a beginner, and I just couldn't help but lift up the rod too soon, pulling the fly right out of the trout's mouth. I tried the age-old practice of visualizing the take, saying "God save the Queen," and then setting the hook, hoping that would help me slow down my set. We switched flies a few times—tried the club sandwich hopper and then back to the chicken hopper, but it didn't make a difference. Way too soon it was 4 p.m. and time to call it a day.

People often ask me if I prefer to be in a boat or wade when I fish. I think I found the perfect solution—when the river permits it. I love standing in the middle of a river, but many rivers can be very difficult to wade because of slippery rocks and large boulders to navigate around, and so mobility and walking distance is limited. On the other hand, I love seeing a lot of a river, which is possible on a drift boat or raft, but there is a certain disconnect when you're not actually standing in the river. And so, when you don't have a river that's moving too rapidly, you get the best of the row vs. wade when sitting in a belly boat.

Chapter 35

The Snake River, Wyoming

August 2013

Five Ranchers and a Cop

The Snake River, Wyoming

Idaho was ablaze with forest fires, and I wasn't sure what I might encounter during the drive to my next fishing destination. I travelled from Boise heading east towards Idaho Falls. About 15 miles east of Mountain Home, the temperature gauge in the Jeep sounded an alarm as the needle jetted to the danger level. Pulling over to the side of the road, I turned off the engine, popped the hood, and watched water boil over from the radiator. Luckily, I'd stopped the car at the crest of a hill where I had cell phone service, and I called AAA. In the next 30 minutes, five ranchers and a cop pulled over, checked on my situation, offered to help and gave me advice about where I should tow the vehicle. It was a broken radiator party! The kind of attention bestowed on me during my car troubles was indicative of the kind of people I met in Idaho throughout the month's visit.

My detour to Mountain Home only cost me about 24 hours. I left the next day for Idaho Falls and the Snake River Campground, where I would catch up on photo editing and writing for several days. Eager to fish another river in Wyoming, I booked my former guide, Derek Hutton, from WorldCast Anglers, located in Victor, Idaho, just west of the Wyoming border. The skies remained incessantly blue, leaving the rivers in the area thirsty as ranchers continued to grab their allotment of river water to keep their animals and crops alive. Thus, many rivers were no longer floatable, and the Wyoming Game and Fish Department closed them to fishing. With this in mind, Derek recommended we drive over to the Snake River Canyon section of Wyoming's Snake River, which was at a higher altitude and, therefore, less stressed. Still in Idaho Falls, I traveled east to Swan Valley, Idaho, where I met Derek. He drove us to our boat launch, which was northwest of Jackson, Wyoming, on the west side of the magnificent Tetons.

The Snake River in Wyoming surprised me in that it was one of the most scenic rivers on my journey. The river was broad and braided bearing long, deep runs. With the Tetons as a backdrop, the sagebrush plateaus, cottonwood and spruce forests and fields of wildflowers left me entranced. The origin of the Snake is found high in Yellowstone National Park, and the river travels 120 miles to the confluence with the Henry's Fork in Idaho. Although water levels were reasonable where we fished, the Snake supplied Palisade Reservoir, which was down 90 percent of capacity.

There are some browns on this river, but mostly two specific species of cutthroats—Snake River fine-spotted cutthroat and Yellowstone cutthroat. In general, cutthroats can be identified by an orange gash under their gill plate, which looks like their throats have been slashed. They are native to the western United States. They are not the vivid, spectacular color of some of the browns and rainbows I have caught, but they are unique and noteworthy.

Derek put his ClackaCraft drift boat in the water close to Astoria Hot Springs, and we floated to the West Lake take-out, just above a whitewater stretch of the river. When we left the boat ramp, we disturbed a team of mergansers that took flight to search for more solitude. I saw a speck on the horizon that was either an eagle or an osprey, and once again, I knew it would be another enchanting day on a river.

Fishing with a "water walker" and a parachute hare's ear, on the first cast, in the first hole, I hooked one of the two cutthroat species—a Snake River fine-spotted cutthroat. However, I rushed the process and reeled too aggressively, losing the fish just before we netted it. Some anglers would count that as a catch, by calling it an "LDR," which means long-distance release. In my case, I actually had an SDR— short-distance release!

The rest of the morning the fishing was slow, but the scenery made up for any piscatorial shortfalls. We ran into a class of beginning kayakers as they made their way through this relatively benign stretch of water, preparing for the next stretch, which presented lots of white water opportunities. Earlier in the summer, I kayaked the Colorado with my sister, Susan, and my two granddaughters, Megan and Lizzie. That stretch of water was also relatively mellow, but there were some tricky spots, as my sister found out with my granddaughter Lizzie, an 8-year old. Instead of riding the rapid to one side, Susan paddled through the center and flipped the boat, right on top of Lizzie, who was a real trooper with just a few tears as she climbed back into the boat after the dunking. Nothing like vacations with grandmas and aunties!

Around noon, Derek banked the boat for a field trip to a side channel that was wide, but too shallow to float. We hiked a half-mile through pink, purple and yellow wildflowers and chirping grasshoppers in the heat of an August afternoon. Several small riffles flowed into some large pools that looked promising, especially since other anglers floating the river ignored the channel. I noticed Derek's face light up when we reached a hole that had a tree hanging over the

water and a dendritic log angled to the middle of the river. He had previously caught a beauty in this hole, but warned me that I had to get my cast right on the first try. I looked at him and said, "Wishful thinking!" Amazingly, I made a near perfect cast, but I was so surprised that by the time I saw the fish rise to eat my fly, I set the hook too late and missed it. We stayed there for at least another 15 minutes trying to get the fish to eat again. Not...talk about frustrating!

Fishing was slow the rest of the morning, but the scenery made up for any piscatorial shortfalls.

I did redeem myself, however. On the way back to the boat, Derek pointed out another small channel that meandered through a copse of trees before reaching the main river. Basically, he wanted me to "thread a needle," by throwing a fly up an impossibly narrow stream to the top of a short riffle. Taking the challenge, I started with a few shorter casts to gauge how much line I should let out, and then I went for it. The fly landed gently on the water, floated unimpeded for about eight inches, and then a fish exploded out of the water to take my fly! I danced with it for several minutes before finally netting a 12-inch fine-spotted cutthroat. *I have always loved field trips!*

That was the highlight of my day as the afternoon brought muddy water and impossible fishing. I didn't see a Yellowstone cutthroat, but I would eventually remedy that. I can't begin to describe the jagged wildness of the Snake River. I thought of Ansel Adams' famous black and white photograph of the Snake and the Tetons and felt privileged to have visited and also photographed this scenic and rugged country.

Chapter 36

The Madison, Montana

September 2013

Sex Dungeons and More

The Madison, Montana

I entered Montana from northeast Idaho, excited to be spending the month of September in perhaps the most famous state for fly-fishing. Crimson fireweed covered the fields; I love this herb because it is one of the first to return after a fire—it's a sign of hope after death. I imagine we will see a lot of this plant in Colorado in the years to come, since 2013 has been one of the worst fire seasons.

Friends had recommended the Slide Inn as *the* place to camp, and it turned out to be a gem. The Slide is located on the upper Madison with an expansive view to the north and the Madison range to the east. The Slide took its name from the rockslide that occurred after the 1959 earthquake that caused the Madison to be naturally dammed by forming Quake Lake.

Perhaps the most interesting aspect of the Slide is its owner, Kelly Galloup—an angler, master fly-tier, author and fly-fishing celebrity. Although I didn't have the nerve to do it, some mutual friends told me to introduce myself by asking him about his "f*!#ing" articulated streamers! When we met, and I told him this, he had a belly laugh and quipped, "That would be great coming from a librarian." Little did he know of the wild and crazy reputation of librarians! Kelly's articulated (two hooks) streamers are a work of art with bodacious names like Sex Dungeon, Stacked Blonde, Butt Monkey and Barely Legal, thus the earlier profanity…you need to have a sense of humor with Kelly. I spoke at length to Kelly about fishing, tying, writing and publishing. We discussed the pros and cons of going with an established publisher or self-publishing. In the end, Kelly's advice stuck—I self-published.

As I walked around the campground, I noticed a growing number of dried seedpods, ragweed and pinecones. The weather was transitioning to fall, requiring my heater in the morning to fend off the chill. I reflected on the last eight months, amazed at how quickly the time had passed.

I spent my first day sequestered in the camper writing and editing photos. I knew people wondered about me when I didn't leave my camper for a day or more. I'm sure it was hard to imagine how a bathroom could possibly fit into a 13-foot trailer! When I finally emerged, people would kindly approach me, asking about the *52 Rivers* signage on my vehicles, and I gladly explained about my trip.

During the previous two weeks, fishing had been tough because of no rain, low flows, hot temperatures and marginal casting. Although weather was certainly a factor when fly-fishing, I also knew that precision casts, an effective hook set and a keen knowledge of the insects on the river mattered more. All of these factors had to coalesce to be successful. It was a humbling time for me because I realized how much more I needed to learn.

On my second evening at the Slide, I meandered over to the east end of the property where you can wade the Madison. I met some Swedes who were touring the western United States on a fly-fishing vacation. Sara and Joachim gave me a beautiful purple fly that resembled a prince nymph. They had killed that spot the previous evening with the purple fly and gave me one to try. I watched Joachim hook a brown and then left to get my rod and experiment with the new fly. We later became Facebook friends, and I hope to fish with them in Sweden one day.

When I returned with the new nymph on my line, I had the spot to myself. I worked the run from top to bottom and back again with the new purple fly. I was about to give up and try a different fly when I saw the indicator disappear into the river. I set the hook and easily netted a small, but richly colored rainbow trout. Thanks, Joachim and Sara!

Arriving back at the Scamp, I was surprised to see that thunderclouds had rolled in while I had been focused on fishing. Several fellow campers and I watched a storm approaching from the west. The colors were magnificent—a mixture of pinkish orange from the sunset as well as grey-blue from the storm clouds. The virgas made it clear we would get some much needed rain, and I would have the pleasure of falling asleep to a symphony of rain drops hitting the fiberglass roof of my camper.

When I awoke the next morning, the rain had ceased, but storm clouds still surrounded us. My guide, Joe Moore, picked me up at the Slide. Joe was raised in Quincy, Illinois, on the Mississippi River. He now lives with his park ranger wife in West Yellowstone. At 8 a.m. with rain gear in hand, Joe and I headed to Lyons Bridge, the first boat launch on the upper Madison.

We started dry-fly fishing with a chubby Chernobyl ant and a golden stone fly while we talked about life on the Madison. Joe rowed a mile downriver and then hopped out of the boat, instructing me where to cast. He walked the boat up and down the river to put me in a perfect position to fish the trout-infested run again and again. That was a first! I picked up several nice rainbows on both flies. (No wonder I caught so many fish when I had a guide.) Once he began rowing again, I tried the undercut banks, with less success. Off to the east, storm clouds looked ominous, but we didn't pay much attention until the first droplets began falling. There's something both delightful and crazy about sitting in a boat on a river in the middle of a downpour. The storm came quickly and ferociously, and we saw a few streaks of

lightning off in the distance. Seconds later there was a deafening clap of thunder just over the next ridge, and Joe looked at me and said, "I think you better put your rod tip down." Duh! Fortunately, from that point forward, we only had to deal with rain.

...the smells were most noteworthy— wet sage, rain-drenched soil, water- logged trees and clean, fresh air.

We delayed lunch, hoping for a break in the weather, which we had—at least for an hour. Patches of blue sky peeked through the gray storm clouds, so we quickly scarfed our lunch on the boat while we could. In Montana, we would be considered trespassers if we stepped above the "high water line" on the banks, which in Joe's mind meant you needed to keep your feet wet. So, lunch on the boat was the norm. Just as we packed up, the rain started again.

Joe tied a streamer on my line, hoping to catch a fish down low while it rained, but the fish were not having any of it. We didn't see another fish that afternoon—hard to believe on the famed Madison.

We drifted by Sun Ranch, formerly owned by Steven Seagal, but now with new owners. This 29,000-acre ranch lined the east side of the river for miles and was one of the properties that prevented development on the river. Everything glistened after the rainfall, and the scenery was magnificent, but the smells were most noteworthy—wet sage, rain-drenched soil, waterlogged trees and clean, fresh air. There was no other place I would have rather been.

North Fork of the Tongue, Wyoming

September 2013

Perfect Recipe

North Fork of the Tongue, Wyoming

Fishing and exploring rivers had become such a priority that I had neglected my writing for nearly a month except for a day or two here and there. I planned to spend ten days at Osen's RV Park and Campground in Livingston, Montana, to hunker down and be productive. As I drove through this charming town with its western storefronts, organic restaurants, and nearby rivers, I knew I would be easily distracted, because there was so much to explore.

Shortly after settling in, a fishing friend told me about an opportunity to fish the North Fork of the Tongue in northern Wyoming—a mere seven-hour drive. It was Labor Day weekend after all, and I decided I should celebrate the beginning of fall. Driving the back roads in order to stay away from Interstate 90, I encountered fields of rolled haystacks and sunflowers.

Internet and cell phone service were nonexistent—I had definitely slipped away from the modern world, and loved it.

The allure of exploration compelled me to make the side trip. I have always wanted to be an "explorer," whatever that means in this day and age. For me, explorers search for challenges that push them outside of their comfort zone to further understand themselves and the world. In many ways, I fit the definition of an explorer as explained by Mikael Strandberg, National Geographic's 2002 Explorer Hero. Says Mikael, "An explorer is somebody who often makes dangerous, difficult, and unique journeys for the main purpose of bringing back news...." Perhaps I could call myself an

"explorer-in-training!" And so, without much thought, I left the camper and writing materials behind and drove east across the state of Montana and south into Wyoming near Sheridan to explore a new river for a few days.

To be honest, I had never heard of the North Fork of the Tongue River. In fact, I had only fished two rivers in Wyoming up to this point because there were so many other rivers that were better known to me. Wyoming does have a reputation for being extremely windy and thus challenging to fish, and perhaps that influenced me when I planned the itinerary for my year of fishing. The bad news about not fishing more Wyoming rivers is that I missed out on a lot; the good news is that I still have a lot to look forward to.

Turning west from Sheridan, I followed the two-lane road until I reached a rather funky fishing and hunting lodge where I had a cabin reservation. In another couple months, the road past this lodge would be closed except to snowmobilers. The cabin had a single light bulb overhead that cast eerie shadows throughout the room. There was one uphol-stered chair that was incredibly lumpy, just like sitting atop a camel, and one wooden hardback chair with no cushion, and no other furniture in the living area. As I settled in for the first evening, I thought I would just sit on the floor to read, but then I noticed the mouse turds underneath me and wondered about Hantavirus, concluding the wooden chair would have to work. Fortunately, I had come to fish, not hang out in the cabin, and the main lodge offered good food and a clean bathroom, so time in the cabin would be limited. Internet and cell phone service were nonexistent—I had definitely slipped away from the modern world and loved it.

The next morning, I drove past beautiful meadows of thick grasses that had taken on fall hues of rust, ochre and gold. I had been warned by several people to keep an eye out for moose, which can be more dangerous than bears. I recalled a story about a friend's encounter with a moose that he claimed inspired him to walk on water as the animal pursued him.

Driving past the first few access points to the river, I found a spot with only one other vehicle. Even though it was September, I wanted to make one last stab at wet-wad-ing even though the predicted high temperature was only 65. I rigged my rod and walked to the river all the while talking and singing to myself so as not to surprise any resident animals.

The North Tongue was appropriately named—the river offered lots of tasty treats. The fish were abundant, the hatches still present (even though it was over 6,000 feet), the wading easy, few anglers and the scenery remarkable. It was a perfect recipe for catching lots of fish. But, just like a perfectly constructed soufflé that falls flat, I only caught one fish on the Tongue. Part of that had to do with my cast-ing slump, which continued; part of it had to do with the fact that the fish just weren't eating (or believing in the fly I presented). To remain positive, I did catch a beautiful cut-throat on a dry fly, and that made the day.

While on the river the first day, I met a man from back east. Like many anglers, he found solace on rivers and in fishing. He was recovering from health problems and as trite as the expression "when it rains, it pours" may be, it aptly applied to the challenges presented to him. We fished together, shared life stories, and watched another angler and his dog on the river...making me yearn to have one. The black lab was 3 years old and as lovable and talented as Lassie or Rin Tin Tin. Watching her in action on the river was remarkable; she stood still for as long as it was necessary for her owner

to catch a fish so that she could then sniff it and join in the experience. I later watched her back outside the cabins where she would sit for ten or 15 minutes without moving anything but her nostrils after she treed a squirrel high up in the branches of a pine tree. Dogs, rivers, fish, blue skies, mountains—now, there's a recipe for contentment.

On the second day, I drove to the South Fork of the Tongue where I found the water very shallow and nearly stagnant. There were fish in the deeper holes, but they were surely stressed from the lack of oxygenated water. I opted to leave them alone, and returned to the North Fork. Once again fishing was slow, and within a couple hours gray storm clouds moved in and the temperature dropped into the 50s. Surprising myself by packing up my gear and leaving the river early, I headed back to the lodge to watch a football game, of all things. I hadn't watched a game in years, and that, along with a few cocktails seemed like a perfect way to spend a Sunday afternoon. Even explorers need a break once in a while.

I loved this river and still intend to return. If you have a yen for some wide-open country and solitude, Wyoming is the place to go. And the writing? I found time for that later.

Chapter 38

Yellowstone River, Montana

September 2013

A Hungry Osprey and a Hardy Woman

Yellowstone River, Montana

I saw the Yellowstone River for the first time in December 2011 after flying to Bozeman, Montana, to scout for rivers to include in my *52 Rivers* journey. During that trip, I drove east to Livingston and headed south, passing three famous spring creeks—DePuy, Armstrong and Nelson's. Just south of the spring creeks in the aptly named Paradise Valley, I found the Yellowstone River between the Absaroka Mountains to the east and the Gallatin Mountains to the west. The river appeared to be composed of millions of diamonds as it reflected the winter sun. I followed its path south until arriving in Gardiner, one of the entrances into Yellowstone National Park. There was no doubt this river would be part of the itinerary.

The Yellowstone is the longest undammed river in the lower 48, and starts its journey in the heart of Yellowstone National Park in northwest Wyoming. After leaving Paradise Valley, the river flows east for 692 miles until it feeds the Missouri. Visiting the area where Lewis and Clark and Sacagawea explored over 200 years ago was inspiring. I wondered how I would have managed as a frontier woman—the thought was probably much more romantic than the reality.

It was hard to believe 20 months had passed since I first visited Yellowstone. After the side trip to the Tongue, I returned to Osen's RV Park in Livingston, excited about meeting my Yellowstone River guide. In the meantime, I wrote prolifically and discovered the Yellowstone Fly Shop, just a five-minute walk down the road. This was very dangerous—I can't seem to walk into a fly shop and not buy something! I had just read an article on the results of the fly shop's "shoot-out." The shoot-out was an annual event where guides and experts gathered to test rods and reels. It made sense that I should spend an afternoon casting their top-rated rods...I had been lusting after a 4-weight rod,

and my birthday was only a couple of weeks away! It was great fun to practice casting for an afternoon, and I discovered that I preferred a soft rod to a stiff one (no metaphors intended), which I had been using the last four years. When all was said and done, I agreed with their conclusion that the Hardy Zenith was the best rod for me.

Through another outfitter in town—Sweetwater Fly Shop—I booked a well-known guide on the river, "Tony V." Finally, it was time to float the Yellowstone! I met Tony behind the fly shop, climbed into his truck and headed south to the Carbella access, where we would start our float. The day was picture-perfect, a nice change from the continuous rains over the last few weeks. We immediately discovered we had something in common—we both grew up in the "Big Peanut." Having shed our New Jersey accents and embedded ourselves in the beauty and vastness of the Rocky Mountain states, each of us had found happiness and peace in these mountains and on the rivers, and never looked back.

Tony wanted me to see as much of the river as possible, so he planned a 16-mile float. The river had a cobbled bottom, and on top it alternated between deep holes and long riffles. We took advantage of fishing dry flies, and he set up my line with a double dry fly rig that included a variation of a drake and a kind of doctored grasshopper that looked more like a honeybee.

Ospreys patrolled the skies in Paradise Valley, and we regularly pointed them out to each other—along with the golden and bald eagles and Canada geese. Ospreys have a wingspan of five to six feet and can fly at speeds close to 200 mph! Although I spotted them numerous times throughout the year, I commented to Tony that I had never seen one dive to catch a fish. Literally, ten seconds later, we were tongue-tied

after spying one hovering over some water 50 yards downriver from us. We watched it fold its wings to its side and begin a steep dive into the water, creating a sensational splash. Then, with a fish tightly clenched in its sharp claws, it flew off, leaving us awestruck.

Although intellectually I knew that fishing every week for eight months would not make me an expert angler, I still hoped that I would be the kind of person who mastered casting quickly. During the last two months, I realized that I had a long way to go to become a precision caster. I had some successes, but I didn't feel confident that I could make the right cast at the critical moment to successfully catch a fish. All of the guides had been extremely helpful, but they each had a little different take on mastering the cast. All the advice and guidance seemed to confound and complicate things for me on the Yellowstone.

After 25 years, Tony knew where the fish were, but I had to aim and shoot the cast precisely, and I was failing miserably. What was I doing wrong? First I became frustrated, disgusted and angry. Then I tried excuses like, "Each guide I've worked with tells me something different." This was true, but for good reasons—the rivers were different or the weather played a factor. Finally, I accepted that this was not my day to cast well or catch fish, and I would need to work harder to become a really good angler. Eight months does not make an expert fisherwoman. On the positive side, I caught some Yellowstone cutthroats, a first for me. I was thankful just for the fact that I had a "first." There is no place for pity on a trout stream.

Looking back on this day, I overanalyzed and overthought everything. The more I thought about casting, the more I failed. I even closed my eyes to "feel" the cast instead of

thinking so much about it; I changed the grip on my rod; I pulled my elbow in closer to my body; I 'broke' my wrist in the back cast; I tried a single haul, then a double haul. In the end, it was just not meant to be. Perhaps the anticipation of fishing this river with such a great guide undermined me. But, that is what makes fly-fishing so attractive to me. It's such a metaphor for life: constant change, highs and lows, successes and failures. If you can fly-fish, you can handle life.

Dusk fell rapidly creating deep shadows mixed with pale pinkish-yellow clouds. By the way, I love the Hardy 4-weight rod I received as a birthday gift from my husband.

Chapter 39

The Jefferson, Montana

September 2013

Eye Candy

The Jefferson, Montana

In a snap of the fingers, the season suddenly changed from summer to fall. The temperature dropped near to freezing at night, although by noon I had to shed clothing. With 78 rivers in Montana, I obviously didn't have enough time to fish them all, so I left a couple weeks without definitive plans to see if circumstances would guide my choice of rivers. Northeast of Bozeman, Montana, I visited the Missouri Headwaters State Park where the Jefferson and the Madison Rivers meet to form the official beginning of the Missouri River. (The Gallatin also intersects the Missouri, a little farther downstream.) It turned out the Jefferson became a good option so I contacted a reliable source, Dave McGee, to recommended a guide.

My husband flew in from Denver to join me, and on the morning of the float, we drove to The River's Edge fly shop in Bozeman to meet our guide, Brett Seng. I entered the shop and was directed to a man facing a display of leaders and other fishing necessities with his back toward me. When I approached him to introduce myself, he turned around in his powder blue fishing shirt, dark hair, 6'2" muscular build, and mirrored shades. I was astonished at his good looks. Wait a minute...I'm supposed to be focusing on the fishing not the guide! I went back outside to "get a grip" and put the gear in his truck, and I told my husband that there was "eye candy" attached to this river float. As it turned out, Brett was a model for fishing magazines as well as a great guide.

We headed west to the Three Forks area where Brett had a favorite spot to start our float after four-wheeling on a two-track to reach the river. After several weeks of rain, the river looked remarkably clear. Just a few weeks back, there were restrictions on fishing the Jefferson because it was so low, but by this time, all the restrictions had been lifted. The riverbanks and countryside had turned shades of

ochre, umber, sienna, rust and slate, and we saw only two other boats all day. It felt like we had become part of a John Constable painting.

We hoped for some fall hatches, but didn't see one all day. It was past the time for dry-fly fishing so nymphs were the plan for the day, although Brett instructed us to handle our lines as if we had a couple of streamers instead of nymphs. He rigged our lines with a stonefly nymph and a worm imitation and had us casting into the un-fishiest looking areas that I've ever seen, twitching our flies and stripping in our lines. And that's the trick of the Jefferson—handle nymphs like streamers and don't fish typical fish habitats. In other words, if pocket water, riffles and undercut banks are the fish equivalent of gated communities on a river, these fish preferred the shantytowns.

The Jefferson is known as a brown trout fishery with few sizeable rainbows. Back in the late 1980s, the Jefferson, like so many other Rocky Mountain rivers, suffered from whirling disease and dewatering problems, which affected the rainbow population, but from what we saw, it had made a good turnaround. I lost myself in casting, mending line, stripping, retrieving and repeating the rhythmic process. We caught a lot of browns in the morning as Brett rowed us to productive spots. We saw a few small rainbows, silvery in color—very few with the vibrant colors that I was used to—but lived mostly with brilliantly colored, near-spawning browns.

About midday, the clouds began to form over the not-too-distant Tobacco Root Mountains. After stopping for lunch, we readied our rain gear, determined to enjoy as much of the day on the river as possible. Brett indicated that there were some productive undercut banks downriver and to get ready for tight lines. Florian decided to go with a hairy, yellow streamer.

moved in from the west. The wind picked up to 20 mph gusts, and we laughed at the fickleness of the day, enjoying a beautiful rainbow. The Jefferson epitomizes the challenge in trying to keep our rivers healthy at the same time meeting agricultural and recreational needs. Because ranchers have maintained their water rights, established as far back as the 1860s, there needs to be a drought management plan put into place. In the case of the Jefferson, I was told that 1/3 of the river's water is diverted into one company's irrigation ditch. (I researched this, but didn't find any evidence.) I don't pretend to understand water law, but I support the work being done on Colorado's new Water Management Plan, because Colorado faces the same water issues as all the western states.

Finally my casting woes seemed to subside—I felt more relaxed and stopped trying to analyze every movement. I hooked a 16-inch brown with bright red spots and a deep caramel color. No sooner had we released that fish than my husband's fishing line tightened. At first, the fish seemed typical of most of the fish we caught that day—in the 14-inch range. However, we soon realized this fish was a step above the norm. The fish leaped several times attempting to be freed of the hook, but when finally netted, it measured 22 inches! I think Brett was more excited than my husband. In fact, I think he was disappointed that he hadn't caught the fish himself! The fish had a wide girth, and its color was more rainbow-like than the bland silvery color of our few earlier bows. We were careful to get him back into the water in a timely way, although we carefully took advantage of the photo opportunity.

The rest of the afternoon passed by quickly, but the horizon provided a changing kaleidoscope of colors, as a storm

Chapter 40

The Blackfoot, Montana

September 2013

A Bunch of Bull

The Blackfoot, Montana

I thought of Norman Maclean's book, *A River Runs Through It,* as I headed west from Bozeman to fish the Blackfoot and Bitterroot rivers near Missoula. I had made a reservation at the Angler's Roost RV Campground in Hamilton, about 60 miles south of Missoula. Having both read Maclean's book and watched Robert Redford's movie rendition, I anticipated great things, and wasn't disappointed.

Pulling into Hamilton, I parked my camper and crashed, because I still had an hour's drive to Missoula the next morning to meet my guide, David Hufman, from the Grizzly Hackle fly shop. He had asked me to meet him at the fly shop by 7 a.m. so we could be one of the first boats on the river.

The Blackfoot was the only river on my itinerary where I had a chance of seeing a bull trout.

A bit bleary-eyed, I arrived at the shop in downtown Missoula on time. We followed Route 200 north to River Junction, where we left the highway to follow a two-track that was littered with branches and leaves after a powerful rainstorm from earlier that week. When we arrived at the boat ramp, there was already a boat in the water and shortly afterward, two other boats pulled up. Obviously, this section of the river was special, and it was important to be the first or second boat to the fishing holes—now I understood the 7 a.m. start-time. Our float would end eight miles down the river at Scotty Brown Bridge.

My goal for the day was to see a bull trout. This member of the char family was formerly known as a Dolly Varden, after the Charles Dickens character, although it's now been reclassified. The Blackfoot was the only river on my itinerary where I had a chance of seeing a bull trout. I had heard stories about anglers catching a decent size rainbow or brown trout, and while trying to net the fish, a bull trout would come up and eat the other fish, allowing them to score two on the same cast! Bulls grow up to 41 inches in length and can weigh in up to 32 pounds; they need to eat other fish to sustain themselves!

David rowed about 200 yards before he anchored the boat next to the most productive hole of the day. Because it was early in the morning and the nights were chilly, the fish were probably stacked in the deeper water, so we started fishing with streamers—mostly variations of a woolly bugger. My confidence level with streamer fishing had improved, and with some additional instruction, I handled my line well. In fact, I had a fish on after my first cast! As soon as I started reeling, the fish shot up into the air like a Cirque du Soleil acrobat, dove back into the water and, I realized, it had successfully released the hook. Dang...outsmarted by a trout.

It was only a few casts later that I once again felt that tug at the end of my line, waited a couple of seconds, set the hook, and had another fish. This time, I netted a nice 15-inch brown that I quickly released. I still wanted a bull trout.

Whatever fish were still in the hole were probably getting wise to angler activity, so we were inclined to row to the next hole, but gave it one more try. The first cast was too short, and I couldn't get much action with it, but the second cast landed exactly where I wanted it. I changed the rhythm on my stripping action. I paused a little longer between strips. I slightly swayed the rod back and forth. And then, once again, I felt a distinct tug on my rod...fish on! This fish was a fighter. I kept my rod tip up, and my line taut applying

for the grand slam—a rainbow and a westslope cutthroat. I wondered why he thought I had any control over what fish decided to bite my line. Patiently, I threw several casts and continued with my strip, strip, strip, pause, waiting to feel that tug again. Not ten minutes later, sure enough, another tug. I hoped it would be that westslope cutthroat that I had not yet seen. This fish also remained underwater for a while, so I couldn't tell what I had caught. As it finally rose to the surface, David yelled out, "It's a westslope cutthroat!" Hard to believe, but true! Its tail was heavily marked with small, freckly spots and its coloration was silvery with some yellowish hues and a soft pink belly. This day made up for all those days when I felt as if I couldn't make a decent cast or catch a fish for the life of me. How quickly life can change.

steady pressure, but not too much. Still, the fish wouldn't surface so we could identify it. A good three minutes passed before we got our first glimpse, and to my great pleasure, it WAS indeed a bull trout!

After finally netting it, I was awed by its beauty; the head and mouth were larger than I expected, and its body was covered with yellow, orange and salmon-colored spots—like it had the measles—while its fins were pinstriped in shades of greyish blue and red, with a distinct white border. I took a photo, and quickly released it, so thankful to have finally seen a bull. David moved on to the next fishing hole, but I really didn't care if I caught another fish all day...at least not until five minutes later!

At the next hole, since it was still before 10 a.m., I continued to fish with a streamer rig. I had caught two of the four kinds of trout on this section of the river (brown, rainbow, bull and westslope cutthroat), and David prodded me to go

I still had to catch a rainbow to score the grand slam, and I was competitive enough to take on that challenge. I didn't count how many casts I made throughout the rest of the day, but it was certainly close to five hundred...and I never saw a rainbow. I can't say I was disappointed—I had caught my bull trout, and that was a thrill in itself. Besides, the river was simply beautiful, the weather flawless and the company great.

Maclean's famous quote from *A River Runs Through It* is, "In our family there was no clear line between religion and fly fishing." This quote clearly aligns with one of the main themes of the book—that the natural world in Montana is sacred. At the end of my day on the Blackfoot, I agreed about the sacredness of Montana's natural world, and I certainly understood firsthand how it affects the human spirit.

Chapter 41

The Bitterroot, Montana

September 2013

—

A Bluebird Day

—

The Bitterroot, Montana

The inspiration behind fishing the Bitterroot was to attend a weekend fundraiser for the non-profit organization Casting for Recovery (CFR), an organization that mobilizes women breast cancer survivors to gather together and learn to fly-fish and connect with other women in similar situations. CFR believes that by providing a new experience in beautiful surroundings, healing can occur. It holds retreats in all 50 states, and in some states—like Colorado—two retreats a year. I am so moved by this organization that all I can say is that it is amazing.

I arrived in Hamilton a week prior to the event so I could fish the Blackfoot and explore the magnificent valley between the Bitterroot and Sapphire Mountain ranges, which create a kind of banana belt. This abundant agricultural valley has attracted such notables as Huey Lewis and Charles Schwab.

After my Blackfoot float (see Chapter 40), the first matter of business in Hamilton was to take care of the Jeep. On the way to Missoula, the transfer box for the transmission needed to be replaced (another AAA rescue). The warranty for the new case required a check-up within two weeks. After searching the Internet for car repair shops in Hamilton, I came up with Reliance Auto Repair and made an appointment, thinking I might fall into 'reliable' hands. I drove the mile from south Hamilton to just north of town, parked my car, and walked into the garage. One of the mechanics saw the signage on my car and intercepted me. "Excuse me, are *you 52 Rivers*?"

Surprised, I answered, "Well, yes, I'm Shelley, and I'm writing a book about 52 rivers. You know about my journey?"

"Oh yes!" he said. "A friend of mine from California told me about what you're doing, and I've been following your blog—trying to figure out a way to do this myself!"

Mike Sharrow turned out to be one of the high points of my week in Hamilton. He took me under his wing and showed me some fishing hot spots, and he's a damned good car mechanic and avid fisherman himself. While we stood chatting in his shop after he finished servicing the Jeep, he said, "Before you go, let me make a phone call because I really want you to meet my friend, John Faust."

Minutes later, I drove to the Faust residence for coffee and donuts. John may not be a German protagonist, but he certainly is a fly-fishing legend in these parts, having been a guide and owner of his own fly shop. He created several flies including Freddie, Freddie Junior and the well-known "Ugly Rudimus."

John was also famous for his mechanical trout, a 22-inch rainbow named Fernando, made of lead and fiberglass. Fernando could rise up to the water surface like a real fish and appear as if it was going after a fly. Fernando and John became famous when his wife, Elna, received a phone call at their fly shop from someone who identified himself as Robert Redford. Elna responded, "Yeah, right! And I'm Sharon Stone!" She didn't believe it was Redford until he mentioned that he needed Fernando for his upcoming movie, *A River Runs Through It*. Later, with Redford's identity confirmed, negotiations started, and Fernando became a movie star! Next time you watch the movie, look for Fernando in the famous Brad Pitt casting scene. I spent several hours with these welcoming and interesting people and purchased a beautiful, handcrafted, monogrammed fly box for my husband.

I floated the Bitterroot twice that week—the first time with Jack Mauer, who was responsible for organizing guides for the upcoming CFR float event. On our half-day together,

Jack turned me on to some great fishing holes including one where I caught one of the most vibrant-looking cutthroats of the year. Jack and I were reveling in our success when all of a sudden I felt my rod dip.

Suddenly, Jack said in a staccato voice, "Don't. Move. Your. Rod. Stand still!"

Photo by Jack Mauer

Of course, I glanced in the direction of my rod and saw a gorgeous mountain bluebird perched on its tip. It looked as surprised as we were, and if it could have spoken, I'm sure it would have said, "Holy shit! Now what do I do?" Jack reached for his camera, but the bird flew away before he could get a shot. We both sat there with our mouths open. We will have to rely on our mind's eye to recall that once-in-a-lifetime image.

I spent the week exploring the Bitterroot, checking out local coffee shops, writing and shooting photos. The CFR event opened with a Friday night gala at the beautiful Ratcheson home, where I joined other folks from around the country, including breast cancer survivors, guides, philanthropists and my fishing partner for the next day, Mary Patry from New Hampshire. A cancer survivor, Mary and I shared stories like old friends and made arrangements for our morning rendezvous to float the Bitterroot with a volunteer guide.

Awakened the next day at the crack of dawn by some chipper robins, I was happy to have some extra time to enjoy the solitude of the early morning. I thought of all the women in my family who have struggled with breast cancer—my mother, aunt and sister—and wondered why I had escaped that challenge...at least up to this point. Mary arrived by 9 a.m., and we met our volunteer guide, Russell Parks from the Missoulian Angler, who started our float behind the campsite where I was parked.

The plan for the day was a "One Fly" contest between the 20 participants. This was a first for me, but I learned that the rules called for us to choose only one fly to fish with throughout the competition. The person who stuck with the same fly for the longest time and caught the most fish was the winner. Russell tied a girdle bug onto Mary's line and a San Juan worm on mine (my choice). With no takers for the first hour, I became impatient and took off the worm, disqualifying myself. On the other hand, Mary kept on her bug for several hours and caught some fish, but we learned in the evening that the winner for the day never changed her fly once and caught quite a few fish with it. The winning fly for the day was a "Jawbreaker"—a custom, hand-tied streamer, tied just that morning by guide Eric Ederer of Renegade Fly Fishing Outfitters.

I took some great photos and, to my delight, won the prize for the best photo of the day—a shot of the river and the Bitterroot Mountains. The day flew by, but not before we had a double catch—Mary with a whitey and me with a rainbow. We kept Russell busy and learned so much from him—he was one of the best teachers I had all year.

Early in the evening we followed a long, meandering driveway with overhanging trees and manicured meadows to the Stock Barn, a private club owned by Charles Schwab. This classic Montana lodge was decorated with western-themed paintings, leather furniture, mounted animals, beautiful carvings and statues, and Native American rugs and baskets. In this historic setting, Peg Miskin, National Program Director, put together an evening to remember with five-star food, fun prizes for the day, and a fabulous silent auction—always remembering why we were there. The time I was involved with CFR supporters deeply moved me. I have found an organization that I want to help fund and donate my time to.

Roaring Fork River, Colorado

October 2013

Honey Hole

Roaring Fork River, Colorado

After spending a month in Idaho and six weeks in Montana, I steered my camper toward Denver and thought about the adjustments I would need to make back at home, even though I would only be there for two weeks before leaving again—this time for New Mexico. Since my departure in early February, I had only returned home for four weeks, and I felt like a different person (especially with my new ponytail)! Throughout the year I had various experiences that pulled me towards making a complete lifestyle change (like moving or starting a new career), but for one reason or another, I didn't follow any sudden, new path aside from the one I was already wandering down. Of course, I would be a different person after this year anyway, but what that meant I would have to find out.

Nearly two decades ago, I had the same feeling after enrolling in an immersion program for seven weeks in southern France to prepare for a teaching position. While in Avignon in Provence, I became so accustomed to a different lifestyle—a new way of dressing, eating, even thinking—that I thought people wouldn't recognize me when I returned to the states. Silly me.

For now, I actually enjoyed some of the conveniences waiting for me at home. My king-sized bed felt really good along with the luxury of a good bath and the conveniences in the kitchen seemed lavish in comparison to the Scamp's two-burner stovetop and no oven or microwave. On the other hand, it felt very complicated—much more to clean and take care of instead of the simplicity to which I had now become accustomed.

I wanted to fish at least one river in Colorado during this time at home again. The Roaring Fork River near Glenwood Springs seemed like the best option—it was only three hours away, and the fishing was still good. I had tried to fish this river earlier in the year, but spring runoff had made the river too muddy.

Photo by Florian Walchak

The Roaring Fork is aptly named for its steep gradient that causes fast and dramatic flows. It is one of the few remaining free-flowing rivers in the state, originating in the Rocky Mountains near Aspen and joining the Colorado River at Glenwood Springs. Similar to most of the rivers in the Rockies these days, the Roaring Fork was very low due to drought and high temperatures.

Throughout the year I had found great guides through my network of angler friends, especially Pat and Carol Oglesby, but this time, I would need to find a guide myself. In January, I had simply Googled pertinent search terms to find a guide and ended up with a 50 percent success rate. This time I called the Fryingpan Anglers, an outfitter that

I previously used when fishing its namesake. They hooked me up with Chris Thomsen, who split his time between guiding on the river and managing a restaurant in Aspen called Pinons. He agreed to float me down the lower section of the Roaring Fork after the confluence with the Fryingpan and Crystal River. This is also called the "bread and butter" section because it's a relatively easy float that offers deep, fruitful runs and is not accessible in many spots unless you are in a boat. We used the boat ramp at Catherine's Store and floated about eight miles.

At the last minute, my husband was able to join me on the float. Unlike my method of learning to fish with a different guide every week, Florian learned to fish on his own. He likes to learn by reading a book and experimenting on his own. He recalled not catching a single fish the entire first year he fished! His experience substantiates the truth that fly-fishing is about so much more than catching fish. To just *be* on a river—with insect hatches, bird sounds, weather changes, wildlife and sometimes fish—is what it's all about. My husband and I are at our best when we're on the river together. We're happy to simply rig our rods, choose our flies and occasionally reel in a fish; however, we do try to follow some basic rules for couples fly-fishing: (1) Set up your own rig or let the guides do the dirty work. (2) Don't poach your partner's drift. (3) Put the camera away. (Oops, I don't do this very well.) Florian also offers this advice in regard to teaching a spouse: "There are three things you should never try and teach your wife—how to drive, how to play golf and how to fly-fish!"

In Montana, I enjoyed autumn at its peak, and now, in Colorado, the season was again in its full glory. I could have spent the entire day just taking photographs, except the fishing turned out to be really good. The contrast between the golden yellow of the aspen and cottonwood trees and the soft red of the oak brush and serviceberry, all reflecting on the water, was as beautiful as any New England fall color trip I took when I was still an Easterner, many moons ago.

Even though we caught several fish, we never saw a hatch all day—although a few bugs came off the water in the afternoon, but nothing to make us believe we would have any success with dry flies. Nevertheless, I tried throwing some for half an hour at one section of the river after we spotted a few rising fish, but didn't have any luck.

Instead, we used a triple nymph rig with a hare's ear on top and a couple of micro-mayflies on the bottom, which caught a combination of browns and rainbows throughout the day. I found my "honey hole" just above the famous "Turkey

Hole," where I caught a good-sized rainbow that took the prize for the day, at least in my mind. After doing some research, I learned that this hole has also been called the "Piggy Pool," which I liked better.

It's interesting how fishing spots get their names. Generically speaking, a "honey hole" refers to that spot on the river where you can be sure to catch a fish. "Avalanche Hole," on the Taylor River, is relatively easy to figure out...I always remained cognizant of my surroundings when I fished there in January (see Chapter 4). The "Toilet Bowl," on the Fryingpan, has to do with of the circular motion of the waters below Ruedi Reservoir. "Stinky Beaver," on the Eagle, is named for a long-dead beaver. I never did find out how "Turkey Hole" acquired its name. Maybe fishing is productive around Thanksgiving?

After finishing the float, we stopped for dinner at my favorite restaurant in Glenwood Springs, The Pullman. We got a late start back to Denver and realized Mother Nature had intervened with a weather reality check—it was October in the Rockies, after all. The always-fickle Vail Pass, at 10,662 feet, had received several inches of snow and then the temperature dropped precipitously. When reaching the top of the pass, we encountered an ice-skating rink with accidents dotting the road in every direction. We drove one of the few cars that made it back to Denver without a mishap, but knew we had been lucky. Now, I only had a couple days to repack the camper and head south on my last excursion of the year.

Chapter 43

Conejos River, Colorado

October 2013

Hunting My Own Way

Conejos River, Colorado

The Hunter's Moon ushered in my visit to the Conejos River in southern Colorado on my way to New Mexico. Plans to stay in my camper were thwarted by a cold snap demanding that campgrounds turn off their water to avoid freezing pipes. Winter had already arrived—not surprising at an altitude of over 8,000 feet in the Rocky Mountains. I rented a rustic cabin at Twin Lakes Campground in Mogote and enjoyed the luxury of a bathroom and little kitchenette, albeit no cell or Internet.

I wondered as I gazed at the moon if I had missed my calling. I imagined becoming a fish and game warden, a wildlife biologist or even a hunter! Yes, I wondered what it would be like to hunt, but realized I am too much of a Buddhist to want to kill anything—except maybe a mosquito! I concluded I could hunt by shooting with my camera, instead of a gun, because I just wanted to connect with nature. I felt so content when outdoors, by myself, listening, observing and studying nature. Inspired by these feelings, I read Walter Harding's biography on Henry Thoreau, *The Days of Henry Thoreau, and picked up Thoreau's Walden* once again. Like Thoreau, I questioned whether society is the only place to live.

I never knowingly killed a fish the whole year. I must say that I had planned on doing that once—just to know how to do it—but just couldn't bring myself to follow through. I talked about it a lot and learned from the guides how to kill and gut one. Besides, I buy and eat fish from the grocery store, so I didn't understand my aversion to doing this except that the fish I caught somehow seemed like partners with me on this journey, and I only wished to affect their lives momentarily.

> *I wondered as I gazed at the moon if I had missed my calling. I imagined becoming a fish and game warden, a wildlife biologist or even a hunter!*

There were lots of hunters this time of year, although very few anglers. Everywhere I went I saw camps of mostly guys with their orange hats and camouflage garb. Like me, they appreciated the beauty and uniqueness of the wilderness, but their goals were different…they had come to find some meat to put in their freezers or garner a trophy for their wall.

I was excited about fishing the Conejos—excited about its beauty and bounty. Certainly all the information I read indicated it was one of the best-kept secrets in Colorado. Even though the river is located in a rather remote area (south of Alamosa and west of Antonito), there are more than 60 miles of access to the river. Wanting to fish the most remote, least populated section of the river, I chose the Pinnacles. (It's uncanny how many rivers have a section called "Pinnacles.") Since I didn't hire a guide for this river, I visited the local fly shop, Conejos River Anglers, to get the skinny on current conditions. The water temperature was topping out at around 40 degrees, which meant the fish were probably searching for a deep hole for the winter. *Probably streamers again.*

A little fall color remained on the aspens and scrub oaks around Mogote, but as I drove higher into the mountains, the swaths of yellow Aspen leaves disappeared, and the grass turned a subtle golden color—almost washed-out looking. Once I parked at the South Fork Campground, I hiked a half-mile down to the river in open country, which was a good thing with elk hunting season in full swing. I admonished myself for not bringing a bright orange hat or piece of clothing with me, but felt safe once I started fishing and stayed near the river.

This section of the river offered a classic collection of pocket water, deep pools, and fast riffles. I was told the fish were perhaps as wild as I would see anywhere, meaning that they had not been stocked, and their coloration would be vivid and dense. Fish here have a tough time surviving because of cold temperatures and low winter flows. Short summer hatches provide some significant food for about four months of the year, but fish are known to get about 90 percent of their food from nymphs under the surface. At any rate, this made for excellent fishing during the four summer months because the fish were not picky about what kind of fly (real or fake) they attacked. I hoped to find some fish nymphing or maybe perhaps with a streamer.

I found a perfect-looking hole under fallen timber and an undercut bank where I was sure I would find a 15-inch wild brown or Rio Grande cutthroat. I started with some woolly

buggers on my new 4-weight Hardy rod. (You could not have convinced me ten years ago that I would be asking for fly rods for my birthday.) Without a single take from streamers, I switched to a dry-dropper rig, but again no results. Finally, I tied on two nymphs with an indicator and some split shot, but nothing rose to the occasion. So much for my perfect hole.

An hour later, I headed upstream to a long riffle and surprised myself by catching a couple small, but beautiful browns in the fastest-moving part of the river. (Interestingly, not the normal location for finding fish—the gentler water next to the riffle.) I quickly and carefully returned them to their habitat, leaving them alive and unharmed. There were other locations on the Conejos where Fish and Game had stocked the river with lots of rainbows, but the wild browns were so beautiful, and the area in which they lived was so gorgeous, that I was content to remain up high on the river.

The days were getting shorter now, and before long, the day's light began to fade. When fishing alone, I was careful not to stretch the limits, and so I forced myself to hike up the steep hill to my car. I drove toward Mogote where my warm cabin awaited me. It was too late to fish another section of the river, but I spent some time scouting and shooting photos. This is really a magical spot where you are far away from the beaten path. I think its magic is the fact that it is relatively remote, with some nice fish—not monsters—and some beautiful scenery. I loved the solitude and simplicity of the Conejos. *What a gift!*

Chapter 44

Rio de los Pinos, Colorado

October 2013

Into the Wild

Rio de los Pinos, Colorado

There were a couple other rivers I wanted to explore from my staging ground at Twin Rivers Campground. The first was the Rio de Los Pinos in the Cruces Basin Wilderness. The second was the "River of No Name" (more on that in Chapter 45). Fishing-wise, the Rio de los Pinos is not known as one of the top fisheries, and it is exactly this fact that made it a gem—while fishing, we never saw another person all day. My husband met me at the cabin so that we could fish the next couple of rivers together. To reach the Los Pinos, we drove 30 miles through ridged dirt roads past numerous camps of hunters. Huddled around campfires, beers in hand, and engaged in discussions and laughter, the hunters gave us a nod and the western version of a wave—the one finger up (and not the middle one)—standard protocol for the backcountry.

Hidden in the mountains, the Los Pinos crosses back and forth along the Colorado and New Mexico state lines. We fished the area known as the Toltec Gorge. The nearest town to this section of the river was Osier, an old railroad settlement and currently a train stop along the Cumbres and Toltec Scenic Railroad. Osier provides train passengers with a lunch along their scenic excursion and a glimpse into the past. An old rope noose, dangling from one of the eaves of a weathered building in the settlement, established in 1880, recalled scenes from TV Westerns I watched late at night in my childhood. We saw anglers disembark at Osier to fish for the day.

We drove to Osier rather than take the train. Praise the engineers who invented 4-wheel drive! At Osier, the road became challenging enough that the four-wheel drive function on my Jeep became essential. Some of the potholes were so large that Florian had to steer us close to the edge of the road where a treacherous drop made me, sitting shotgun, think twice about where we were headed. A few miles going this way took a good 30 minutes, and I wondered if we should have just parked at Osier and hiked down.

We met another carload of anglers from New Mexico where the road eventually dead-ended at the river. Coincidentally, I had just discovered an angling book on New Mexico entitled *49 Trout Streams of New Mexico* by Raymond C. Shewnack and William J. Frangos—sounding remarkably similar to my book. One of the guys had actually co-authored the book! We exchanged writing and publishing stories until we realized the morning was slipping away. They headed upstream, and we headed downstream, and our paths didn't cross again for the rest of the day.

We found an idyllic spot—a crystal clear river cascading over lichen-covered boulders, a still robust flow even though it was October, steep banks rising up from the river with heavy pine and fir forests and grasses, willows and shrubs in their fall attire. I could have simply sat on the banks contemplating life all day, like I used to do in my high school years on the Jersey shore at the Atlantic Ocean.

The Los Pinos is only ten to 15 feet wide for most of the two miles we fished. Access to the river was difficult except in strategic, well-trampled areas, but casting was relatively easy once reaching the banks. Although the stream was between one and four feet deep (with some deeper holes), the wading was difficult due to a slippery bottom of cobblestone and slickrock. Once again, my wading staff came to the rescue.

I grabbed the first sweet hole, which had a rapid run that led into a deep pool, a perfect spot for fish to hole up. I was without a guide and welcomed the chance to test my fly selection, good knots and all the other elements involved with the right rig. I couldn't discern the depth of the hole, so I decided to start with dry flies even though I hadn't seen any hatches occur. If I didn't get any action, I would set up a nymph rig next and end with some streamers. I thought it was a good plan. I probably cast the dry fly for a good 20 minutes before setting up a line with two nymphs. Again, another 20 minutes with no action. On to a nice yellow woolly bugger and another 20 minutes with no luck. Poof! An hour passed. I was appreciative of my surroundings and the practice tying on flies and casting, but was defeated by this hole. Some seasoned anglers wouldn't make more than a couple dozen casts into the same spot before moving on. *Hmmm.*

I bushwhacked through the thick vegetation along the river. The hiking was pretty tough, although occasionally there was the remnant of a trail stomped down by previous anglers. I set myself up again about a half mile farther downstream. The fishing spot had a nice run and should have held some fish. Once again I went through the routine of dry, nymph, streamer. In the meantime, I heard a distant "Woo-hoo!" and knew that my husband wouldn't be skunked on this day. I became disgruntled with this spot and renegotiated my way even farther downstream.

The river had an allure that drove me deeper and deeper downstream. I appreciated the silence and thrill of the wilderness. The ground squirrels that spotted me perked up as if to say, "What are YOU doing here?" The wind moaned through the gorge and made me wonder at the wisdom of being by myself in this starkly uninhabited area. It dawned on me just how far I had wandered from our car, parked in an already remote area. I recalled Jon Krakauer's book *Into the Wild*. It pieced together the chilling details of the life-ending adventure of Christopher McCandless that took place only 15 miles from civilization in Alaska. Due to a "perfect storm" of bad circumstances, McCandless ended up starving to death. This was not the time to let my imagination wander, but it did make me more wary as I hiked up and down steep slopes or waded across slippery rocks in the river.

I had yet to see a black bear (or a moose, for that matter) all year, although I have seen both in previous years. This place suddenly seemed primed to have that happen. In any case, I felt confident and prepared to handle an encounter because (1) I read plenty about what to do and (2) I carried bear spray on a hip belt. (Black bears were a distinct possibility, but seeing a grizzly bear in Colorado is a moot point because Colorado no longer has any grizzlies. However, the last one that had been spotted 35 years ago was seen in the very area where I then stood.) If I did see a bear, could I really avoid eye contact, stand tall while backing away gently, and not freak out? Fortunately, I didn't have to find out on this day. In fact, I was sure these animals would do just about anything to stay as far away from me as possible. One thing I knew for sure, I would not let my imagination of a chance encounter scare me away from wandering about the wilderness.

I didn't fish for the rest of the day and instead shot photos of the wild country. Facing a 60-minute hike back to the car, I found myself, once again, short on time...*time, precious time*.... I remembered my dad saying when he turned 80 that a 24-hour day seemed like only a couple of hours to him. I was 30 years younger than he was when he said those words, and yet I completely understood. How could this whole year be nearly over? It was mind-boggling.

Chapter 45

River of No Name, Colorado

November 2013

—

The Secret

—

River of No Name, Colorado

By this point in the journey, I had fished a few extra rivers so that I would have a choice to include in my book. This allowed some editorial flexibility, and I had the added pleasure of being able to include an extra river here and there that may turn out to be special. The unplanned river for this week turned out to be stellar.

After a long conversation with local anglers at the Conejos River Anglers fly shop, I found myself on the "River of No Name." This was the tag I gave to the river after they asked me not to reveal its name. I understood their reasoning after I fished the river; it was simply not suited for large numbers of anglers. They also said that John Gierach fished the river with one of their guides, and it was an extraordinary place to see. John Gierach is one of my husband's heroes because he has actually managed to make a living fly-fishing and writing books about it. We own over 30 of his books!

Following Gierach's lead, I made arrangements with Troy Smith to take us to the river. A rugged-looking mountain man with a long red beard, he used his four-wheel drive vehicle to get us to the "River of No Name." We parked, and while hiking toward the river, I noticed tracks and scat on the ground indicating that we would share space with coyotes, foxes, bears and mountain lions. I never saw them, but was sure they saw me. I knew I was never really in control of nature, but also felt no danger. Certainly, in this outdoor world, we are much more insignificant and unimportant than we perceive.

Troy is one of the more fascinating guides I met on my journey. I loved how his spare tire served as a holding tank for his used flies. A native of New Mexico and the lead fishing guide at Conejos River Anglers, he is also one of five sanctioned trappers in the state of New Mexico. It was interesting how

I found that out. During a casual conversation at lunch, I asked him, "What do you do during the winter?" His answer was a rather vague, "Oh, I get around a lot." After a minor inquisition (something I'm good at) he answered that he was a trapper. Troy was unsure about my reaction to trapping, so he hesitated at first, but I assured him that I was not judgmental but instead rather fascinated! Fascinated because I didn't realize that trapping still occurred, and I really didn't know anything about it. I don't own a fur coat, but I also wouldn't throw paint on one being worn either.

I have regularly heard how traps are gruesome, inhumane devices that break bones on animals' legs, leaving them to die painfully in the wilderness. This is the furthest thing from the truth—at least with Troy. His traps do not have sharp metal teeth that break the animal's leg; they are coil-sprung, steel footholds, meaning they restrain the animal, but do not hurt it. He wanders the wilderness every day—no matter the weather conditions—and monitors every trap he's set so he can either release animals whose populations are small, or harvest those that are overpopulated. I would love to see how he releases a mountain lion, for example.

The most important question here is...why? Why trap? Troy works closely with the Fish and Wildlife organization in New Mexico to ensure that the number of animals in the wilderness is kept in balance with the food supply in order to serve the long-term health of their population. As Troy said, "Mother Nature can be a lot more cruel than any human being when things get out of whack." Think in terms of deer starving in the winter due to overpopulation. There is a reason for hunting and trapping and wildlife maintenance.

As a librarian and information person, I have learned over and over again to listen to all sides of a story to come up with the facts. It never ceases to amaze me how little I really know. In this case, I gained a whole new perspective on trapping because of this chance encounter. That said, I want to also acknowledge the important work that the animal rights organizations do for the health and well-being of the other creatures with whom we share this planet. Certainly, this is an interesting topic for dinner conversations with friends who enjoy issue-oriented discussions.

Troy has an obvious understanding and awareness of his surroundings. I have never felt safer anywhere, city or mountains, than I did with him. This is a man who's had over 50 bear encounters (mostly spotting them from a distance), but one when he was charged and knocked off his feet, but not otherwise harmed. Troy said it felt like he had been hit by a 2 x 4.

Back to the "River of No Name." As mentioned, I was sworn to secrecy about this stream because it really cannot handle much more than a couple of anglers a day. It was an intimate affair—a river meandering 12 miles next to high bluffs through a canyon, only accessible from either its upper reaches or lower reaches (which we did). The stream was never more than ten feet wide, and the fish were easily spooked, to say the least. I had to make a perfect cast upstream to the fish and then let the drift pass over their heads. It was such a thrill when I did it right. If you spooked them by stumbling, or made a bad cast and scared them, they would disappear for hours—thus, the reason for only a small number of anglers.

Even though it was late October, the dry-fly fishing was phenomenal. There were no hatches, but the fish weren't trying to follow a hatch—they wanted to fatten up before winter and were willing to eat anything that looked buggy.

In some ways, fishing on this stream reminded me of my day in the Pinnacles section of the Strawberry (see Chapter 22)—wild, isolated, lots of fish, technical fishing, secretive and captivating.

I wondered if I could keep the secret. I remembered Benjamin Franklin's quote, "Three can keep a secret if two of them are dead!" There's something about secret fishing holes that presses you to blurt out the skinny. For now, it shall remain the "River of No Name."

Chapter 46

Rio Grande Gorge, New Mexico

November 2013

Converted

Rio Grande Gorge, New Mexico

When the blustery days of November become the norm in the Northern Rockies and the fishing gets tough or shuts down, anglers can prolong their fishing lives in northern New Mexico where temperatures stay warmer and there is less snow. Having said that, the elevation is still around 7,000 feet, so the area is not immune to rivers icing up at night and other difficult winter fishing conditions.

Over the last 15 years, I've had mixed feelings about traveling to New Mexico. My negative feelings were rooted in the time when my husband and I started our second dating cycle in Albuquerque (originally, we were college sweethearts). I really didn't like much about that desert city then—a mass of strip malls and non-stop, unsynced stoplights. Part of that prejudice came from the fact that I had just moved back to Colorado after a 25-year hiatus, and wanted to be sure I stayed firmly planted there. Even with those lingering negative feelings, the rivers I visited with guide Nick Streit changed my mind about everything New Mexican.

Perhaps the most famous river in New Mexico is the Rio Grande, although the San Juan is a close second. I fished the Rio Grande in Colorado in late June during the South Fork Fire (see Chapter 26) and found it quite challenging with all the smoke and associated dangers of the forest fires. Not surprisingly, the Rio Grande Gorge in New Mexico turned out to be a completely different experience. It is one of longest rivers in North America, but interestingly, the river is difficult to access for much of its length in New Mexico. Even the areas where I fished required a hike down a 700-1,000 foot elevation drop that could be challenging for some. The wildness of the river was recognized back in 1968 when Congress designated the Rio Grande Gorge as part of the National Wild and Scenic Rivers system.

I drove the Scamp toward Taos for the last leg of my *52 Rivers* excursion. I was impressed with the majestic Sangre de Cristo Mountains and the rosy-peach sunset as a backdrop. I softened, thinking about why New Mexico is known as the "Land of Enchantment." I picked a camping site north of Taos at the Monte Bella RV Park, a gated community with wonderfully kind proprietors.

For five of the seven rivers I had chosen to fish in New Mexico, I hired one guide, Nick Streit, from the Taos Fly Shop (and now also the owner of The Reel Life in Santa Fe). Fishing with Nick was one of the best recommendations I was given all year—thanks for that, Troy Smith! I first met Nick at his fly shop in Taos—the same location where his father had first opened a fly shop in 1980. We agreed to let the fickleness of the weather and the flows of the rivers determine our schedule for the week. Nick recommended starting our New Mexico tour on the Rio Grande Gorge. After a short drive from the Taos Fly Shop, he parked his truck on a high bluff above the river in a rather remote spot, away from the area that was plagued with a slew of vehicle break-ins. We suited up and started the trek to Mamby Hot Springs, our starting point on the river.

The route down was steeped in natural history, where fractures in the rock revealed the ancient magma deposited 20 million years ago by nearby volcanoes. Like the Colorado River's work through the Grand Canyon, the Rio Grande River carved a deep canyon through the basalt, leaving behind castle-like walls as you look back up from the river. I anticipated a challenging hike that involved a 1,000-foot vertical drop to the river, but it turned out to be relatively easy due to the well-maintained switchbacks. The area is also known as Stagecoach Hot Springs because two Taos merchants in the late 1890s constructed a road that allowed stagecoaches to connect passengers from Taos to the nearest railroad station of the Denver and Rio Grande Railroad. The road, built into the side of the steep basalt cliffs, was an engineering marvel.

If you live for beautiful sunsets and great views, I've got just the place for you...plus, the fishing is fantastic.

The river was surprisingly clear for a late October day. Often, the snow from higher elevations melted during the warmth of the day, muddying up the river, but not on this day. We spotted fish in many of the runs, cast out a dry/dropper rig or a double and even triple nymph rig, and a fish would hit one of the flies. As always, the names of the flies are a story within themselves, and on this day, we ended up with a chubby Chernobyl, a shit fly, and a defrocked micro-mayfly! When using a dry/dropper, very subtle movements of the floating fly indicated a strike below. As always, I was a bit distracted by the rest of the wildlife on the river—marmots, ground squirrels, deer and birds; so many gorgeous raptors including turkey vultures, eagles, red-tailed hawks, northern harriers and prairie falcons—so I'm afraid I missed a few strikes!

Nick pointed out the petroglyphs on the faces of the large basalt rocks that the Anasazi chiseled over 900 years ago. One of the petroglyphs consisted of three concentric circles with a dot in the middle, meaning the Pueblo name of the springs, Wa-pu-mee. In his article, "Soaking in the Land of Enchantment," Craig Martin tells a wonderful story about the springs. "This long-standing name, roughly translated as 'water of long life,' brought Spanish explorers to the area in the sixteenth century. The Europeans were searching for the Aztec's famed spring of perpetual youth, which was said to lie many days' journey north of Mexico City—a rather broad geographical range, but in the hopeful eyes of the Conquistadors, the description was a perfect fit for the Rio Grande Gorge. The Spanish found a well-worn trail from the rim of the canyon to the hot springs, and undoubtedly their pulses quickened. Alas their soak in the water failed to deliver the miracle for which they had come." If not everlasting life, at least they had found a remarkably beautiful spot to soak their bodies.

I have been lucky to have a lot of "firsts" on many of the rivers I fished, and the Rio Grande Gorge provided yet another—a Rio Grande cutthroat. Realistically speaking, this fish I caught was most likely a planted one, but it was cool to see its yellow-green and bronze flanks dotted with a small number of spots. They are not large fish—12 to 15-inches—but who said size matters?

Storm clouds moved in from the west later in the afternoon, and we were thankful that we had chosen to fish the Rio Grande Gorge first, before the river became muddied by rain or runoff. In fact, a deluge of rain hit my campsite that night, and the mountains were powdered with snow the next morning when I woke up. The clouds made for some excellent photo opportunities both that afternoon and the next morning, and Nick loved to take photos as much as I did. Some of his shots have appeared in fly-fishing magazines. It was going to be a great week with Nick.

If you live for beautiful sunsets and great views, I've got just the place for you...plus, the fishing is fantastic. I'm a New Mexico convert!

Chapter 47

Red River, New Mexico

November 2013

You Had to Be There

Red River, New Mexico

After spending a day on a river with a guide, it's not unusual to feel as if you have been lifelong friends. Similar to women's relationships with their hairdressers, clients (both men and women) feel comfortable sharing life stories with their guide as they enjoy the beauty of the outdoors and the thrill of fishing. And so it was with guide Nick Streit and me. We spent five days sharing a love of fishing, rivers, photography and life stories.

When I first spoke on the phone with Nick about my New Mexico plans, I asked about the Red River but detected some hesitation in his voice. He knew I was a "senior" and didn't know whether I would be able to handle the hard hike down to the river and the challenge of wading in it. We had left the option open to fish this river until we spent our first day together on the Rio Grande Gorge, also a serious hike down to the river, just not as difficult as the one to the Red. As it turned out, the Rio Grande Gorge hike was easy for me, so

the Red River became the second river I fished with Nick. Thanks to the Park Service, the switchbacks made the hike easily manageable, even for us 60-year olds!

I remember when my dad turned 60; I traveled back to New Jersey where I grew up, just 15 miles west of New York City, where my father worked for his entire life. When I lived and worked there in my 20s, I loved meeting him for lunch or dinner at a Japanese restaurant, whose name I don't recall, near Rockefeller Center. To revisit the past together, we made the commute through the Lincoln Tunnel into the city to share a celebratory meal at this same Japanese restaurant where we sat cross-legged on cushions on the floor savoring the sukiyaki. At one point during the meal, he looked at me and said, "You know, Shell, I don't feel a day over 30 (my age at the time). How can 60 years have passed so quickly?" Now, 30+ years later, my dad has passed on, and I'm saying the same thing to my 30-year old sons. Not only do I still feel 30, I can still climb down a steep riverbank!

The Red River is quite spectacular because, like the Rio Grande Gorge, it has carved its way through massive basalt cliffs. It is the largest tributary of the Rio Grande, and although it isn't a tailwater, natural springs upstream keep the water temperature a consistent 40 to 50 degrees, allowing for fishing year round. According to the Bureau of Land Management's website, a four-mile section of the Red River, just before its confluence with the Rio Grande Gorge, was designated as a Wild and Scenic River. Unfortunately, there's a dark side to its beauty and wildness. The river has a questionable history due to a molybdenum mining operation that badly polluted the lower river and contaminated groundwater for years. On the positive side, the springs have helped to clean up the river—although I must admit I wouldn't eat any of the fish from it. (Regulations allow an angler to keep five fish a day on the Red.) I didn't see any signs of pollution; in fact, the river was as pretty as any I had fished all year.

We hiked 30 minutes down the 800 vertical foot drop at El Aguaje from the rim at 7,000 feet to this trout haven, a mile north of the confluence with the Rio Grande Gorge. I admired the palette of colors—tans, crimsons, grays, greens and deep yellow as I followed the trail to the river. The fall colors were past their prime, but the scrub oaks were a beautiful deep orange color. The water in the river was gin clear as it gushed over boulders that scattered about. Behind the boulders, the fish found perfect pools to call home. Although the largest fish are found closer to the confluence of the two rivers, the mostly wild brown trout are known to swim up the Red River from the Rio Grande and spawn, creating an abundance of browns for many miles north of the confluence. Each pool offered a pod of fish in the 9 to 15-inch range. The wading was very difficult because of the powerful current, slippery rocks, thick brush along the banks and the steep slopes, but I caught several browns.

I found the perfect lunch—tomato-basil soup with grilled cheese sandwiches. Talk about comfort food! He had hiked down the trail with a burner and all the ingredients to make this special repast. 'Perfect' had started to become the norm for me, but without expectations or lack of appreciation.

We fished until late afternoon, leaving enough time to make it up to the rim before dusk because the sunsets were famously spectacular, cloud cover permitting. As we made our way back up the switchbacks, we could see clouds rolling in from the west—that put a little spring in our step.

Mother Nature treated us to an incredible light show. We arrived at the overlook of the confluence of the Red and the Rio Grande just in time to admire the setting sun. As we looked up and down the remarkable canyon, the sky turned ochre and pink and the clouds puffed up and reflected the waning light. The wind picked up so there was a distinct chill in the air. Hawks and raptors took advantage of the air currents, skydiving and performing flying feats. There was not another human in view. In every direction, the sky presented a kaleidoscope of colors and left us both speechless. We spent an hour along the rim trying to catch the beauty of the moment in a photograph, but that's just not possible. The beauty of that scene is imprinted in my mind's eye more vividly than I could describe or capture it with any camera and display on a computer or piece of paper. You really had to be there.

As we moved to different fishing spots, Nick blazed a trail, hiking like a bighorn sheep, inspiring me to climb up and down the slopes. I was glad that I made it to wherever he went, just a lot slower. After fishing several hours, we arrived at a bend in the river where the brush thinned out and the river slowed, forming a glassy slick. We put down our rods and changed our focus to taking photographs. It was there that Nick offered to do a portrait session with me, which produced the back cover photo for this book.

As always, I felt starved by early afternoon. Nick left me shooting photos by the river and went to set out lunch on a nearby picnic table. I expected the usual fare—a deli sandwich with chips and a cookie. When he called me to the table,

Chama River, New Mexico

November 2013

Carp Down the Scarp

Chama River, New Mexico

The town of Abiquiu, New Mexico, was the home of the well-known artist Georgia O'Keeffe from 1949 to 1986. It is also famous for being the site where movies such as Indiana Jones, City Slickers and Red Dawn were filmed. For me, Abiquiu (pronounced abbey-q) meant the home of the Chama River.

> *The Cliffs are composed of 1.8 billion-year-old granite, which I find remarkable not only because of their age, but also because someone is smart enough to know that.*

Like the Rio de Los Pinos, the Chama begins as a small stream in the San Juan Mountains in Southern Colorado and crosses the border into New Mexico. I'm really eager to follow a river to its origin. In some cases, this may require bushwhacking and a difficult climb, in others—maybe not. When first moving to Colorado, I was surprised to learn about all the "fourteeners" (mountains over 14,000 feet) and the varieties of access to them. Some require a highly technical climb to get to the summit; others, like Mt. Evans, have road access to the top. My goal is to try and find access to a river's origin, Mt. Evans-style!

Together with Nick Streit again, we headed west from Taos on a bluebird day in November, dodging the cold weather bullet. The mountains were covered with newly fallen snow, but otherwise it felt like springtime. The drive took us past the famous rock formation known as the Brazos Cliffs. The

Cliffs are composed of 1.8 billion-year-old granite, which I find remarkable not only because of their age, but also because someone is smart enough to know that.

The Chama runs 120 miles and is the home of three reservoirs: the Heron, El Vado and Abiquiu. After the confluence with the Brazos River, just south of the town of Chama, the river becomes significant. We fished two sections of the river—above and below the El Vado Reservoir. Below the reservoir, access is limited to one spot—Cooper's, a campground with cabins, picnic tables and friendly dogs running around. We paid our $5 daily use fee and observed a handful of bait fishermen working to catch their daily limit. The swaying, narrow suspension bridge across the river is a challenge!

Nick warned me that the Chama is well known for its brownish-gray color due to the ravages of erosion from over-logging Ponderosa Pines in the 19th century. (Hard to believe this is still having an effect.) Observing how murky it was, I didn't think there was a chance of catching a fish, but Nick knew better. We scrambled up the river's bank and then back down to avoid the obstacles in the river. Who needs a gym? When we waded into the river, I was grateful that I had attached my studded boot soles and had a wading staff to lean on, because the rocks were as slippery as black ice.

We stopped to fish some holes behind large boulders. Nick tied on a streamer that looked like a variation of a muddler minnow. I made the cast and followed up with a strip, strip, pause, and immediately hooked the first of several fish out of this hole. Fish took that fly time and again in water that provided little opportunity to be discerning. When you're on to fish, the standard procedure is to stay put. Why go searching someplace else if you're finding fish where you are? On the other hand, you don't want to overfish a spot such that you leave the fish stressed. So, after bringing in a dozen, we moved closer to the El Vado Dam. There, I fished a long run where I pulled out a couple of rainbows. Interestingly, the normal vibrant colors of these fish were missing. The coloration of the fish seemed to match the muddy waters, meaning bland and plain-Jane looking.

Our stomachs began to growl, so we headed back to the campground. Once again Nick had brought a portable burner and cooked up some pasta and served a delicious salad. I sat at a picnic table by the river feeling very spoiled. I love having someone cook for me; my husband loves to cook, and his son, Mike, makes his living as a chef in Denver. One of the reasons I still enjoy cities is because of the restaurant scene.

After our late lunch, we drove upriver to the northern El Vado section of the river near the Heron Reservoir. We arrived mid-afternoon, which meant that the sun was hidden behind the canyon walls, making it chilly and putting the fish down. No matter. We saw a shoal of large carp swimming just below the dam, and decided to spend some time trying

to fish for these cagy rascals. Although more people in the U.S. have taken an interest in carp fishing in recent years, in the UK, there is an enthusiastic carp crowd. "Let's be part of the vanguard!" I announced to Nick.

The bank was about 30 feet high and covered with large boulders. Nick stayed at the top where he could spot the submarine-like fish on the move as I hopscotched down to the river's edge. With Nick coaching me where to cast, I was sure that I was going to have the chance to catch my first carp. Several times, I could hear the excitement in Nick's voice..."Get ready. Here they come; they're following your fly!" And then they would inevitably turn away. I fished for those carp for over an hour. I even made Nick try because I really wanted to see one of them. No luck for either of us.

The afternoon gave way to dusk as we climbed back up the trail to his truck. We slowly made our way out of the backcountry and spotted half a dozen bucks with impressive racks. They didn't spook easily as we stopped for photos; I guess they felt safe on BLM land, even though it was hunting season.

I had started to fall in love with New Mexico...fickle woman that I am.

Cimarron River, New Mexico

November 2013

A Perfect Creation

Cimarron River, New Mexico

Nick and I continued to change our itinerary daily to accommodate the weather, stream flows and our moods. It was hard to find perfect conditions on any river this time of year, but we were content with the reports coming out on the Cimarron. The conditions were good, but not optimum, on the day we drove to the river. The flow was at seven cfs instead of zero from just a few days earlier—at least it was flowing! The weather forecaster predicted a perfect day, warming up to the 60s with brilliant sunshine. Nick warned me that the fishing might be difficult at best. At least I could try, I decided, and besides, I always had my camera.

Cimarron means "wild" in a Spanish botanical context. In some ways, it did seem wild—with steep canyon walls and scruffy forests that looked almost haunted with broken and downed branches. However, the road followed the river for as far as we travelled, which made it difficult to think of as wild.

One interesting fact I learned about the Cimarron is that it flows east to the Mississippi watershed, unlike other northern New Mexican rivers that flow south into the Rio Grande watershed. The river has its share of private and public water, just like all the other rivers I fished, but we stayed on the public land. Casting on the Cimarron can be difficult because of the amount of forestation along its banks. I had become more adept at making a cast that didn't catch the brush; that is, I had it somewhat figured out. If I stood in the middle of the stream and sent the cast right up the middle, it could be pretty effective! *Not rocket science.*

The sun had not yet risen above the canyon walls as we followed the river to our first fishing spot. After parking, we grabbed our gear and walked through a barren-looking grove with lots of stumps and compressed leaves. I felt engulfed in a beige and brown world, except for the deep blue sky.

Nick rigged my line with a parachute adams dry fly. Who would have thought I would be fishing with dries in November? We moved up to the first shallow riffle that ended in a deeper pool and within a few casts, I saw that now familiar splash on the surface that has never ceased to surprise me every time it happens. It took a moment to synch the timing of my hook set with the rises, but eventually I succeeded in grabbing some browns from the hole. They were smallish—around 10 inches—but a beautiful mustard color that matched any jar of Gulden's mustard I've ever bought.

We fished a few other holes before stopping for lunch at a riverside picnic table. Nick had sent me off on my own, and I promptly snagged my line. I hadn't done that all morning, and yet on my first cast by myself, I became entangled. I guess I need an audience to stay more focused and precise. Instead, I took out my camera while stellar jays posed for me,

allowing some great shots. They are such regal looking birds—similar to my own favorite cedar waxwings—looking like the Fonzies of the bird world with their feathered coifs. Nick called me over for lunch, which was gourmet by camping standards; a chicken parmesan dish with a salad, bread and dessert. I always had to fast for a day or two after fishing with guides.

After lunch we drove to a spot a little farther north on the river. It was an open meadow with some fallen trees. The sun was high, the day was warm and the fish were hungry. I learned throughout the year to always look for wood; it was near wood that fish loved to hang out. In this case, a huge branch of a tree had fallen into the river. The problem would be to keep my cast parallel to the water so I could cast under the branches that spread out from the limb.

The fish were very nervous in this open, exposed area, and it was difficult for the two of us to be stealthy. As we waded into the river we watched several large browns hightail it downstream. We assumed there had to be some fish left hiding under the tree branch. I made my first cast and immediately caught my fly on a branch. Nick didn't even sigh, but I grimaced. He miraculously unsnagged it without disturbing the hole and offered me a casting lesson for this difficult approach. We stood in the middle of the river for several minutes talking about the needed cast and how to make that happen. All of a sudden, Nick spotted a big brown just below the tree, feeding in the middle of the river. Due to its size, we knew this fish had been around a long time, so it was unusual that he would be willing to put himself in such a vulnerable position in the middle of the day.

Nick's excitement rubbed off on me as he grabbed my rod and took off the dry fly and put on an egg pattern. He coached me again on the cast and how to land the egg softly. He told me I probably had only one chance to catch this fish. *No pressure.*

My first cast was the right distance, but about six inches to the left. The fish didn't budge. (We assumed it was blind in the left eye.) I got my second cast just right. I waited the one...two...three seconds while it began to drift, drift, drift and then the fish hit. I yelled out, "I got it!" I handled the line with finesse and steadily muscled the fish to the bank. Of course we had forgotten to bring a net, so Nick removed the hook and we held on to the fish at the same time so we could get a photograph—not a practice I would normally recommend, but for a fish as special as this, I had to bend the rules. From mid-belly to its tail fin, the brownie had a red blush on its sleek body as if embarrassed by its beauty. The brown spots were highlighted in red and then had a brownish green halo that encircled them. Its head had a turquoise-green streak leading off its deep brown eyes, and its underbelly was dark mustard yellow. Its fins were the same mustard color but highlighted with white along the edges. It was a perfect creation, in my humble opinion, and I was darn lucky to have had the chance to share a few moments with it.

It turned out to be one of the largest fish Nick had seen on the Cimarron in over ten years. I actually made his website's Fish Friday spot and had several people contact me on my Facebook page to congratulate me. I felt like a real angler. It had only taken a year.

Pecos River, New Mexico

November 2013

Pie in the Sky

Pecos River, New Mexico

Like the Cimarron, I didn't think I was going to have the opportunity to fish the Pecos River, and for the same reasons—low flows, cold weather and few fish. Again, I lucked out with another late winter storm that brought rain in the low country and deposited snow in the mountains, increasing the river flow and offering a chance to fish the Pecos.

The Pecos River is a beautiful, smaller stream that flows south out of the Pecos Wilderness. It is located only 45 miles east of Santa Fe and flows for over 900 miles into the Rio Grande River in Texas. There is a road that follows the stream up to the beginning of a wilderness area where you can hike in to follow the river to its headwaters. The Pecos has lots of pockets, pools and riffles, and is surrounded by high mountain terrain with steep cliffs of sandstone, shale and limestone. The slopes are dotted with fir, pine and spruce, making for an impressive setting.

In 1990, the Feds categorized 20 miles of the upper river, starting at its headwaters in the Sangre de Cristo Mountains, as a Wild and Scenic River. This happened none too soon. Prior to this designation, trout were harvested to a near destruction of the fishery. Now the river is healthy: stocked with rainbows; a good population of browns; catch and release limitations; and a better fishery than ever before. Although the management of our fisheries by Federal agencies is a controversial topic, I believe that they have done a good job. There is a movement to lessen the amount of stocking from hatcheries to allow the wild fish to grow and thrive without competition. I imagine the solution lies in careful oversight of each unique situation instead of blanket decisions.

At Nick's suggestion, I hooked up with Norman Maktima, one of the best guides on the Pecos, and a competitive fly-fisherman on the national scene. Norman has fished the Pecos since he was a toddler. He and Nick have been friends since their teens, when they fished competitively on the first U.SA. Youth Fly-Fishing Team.

Norman said the river had been under a lot of pressure during the summer—too many fishermen, not enough rain. I selfishly hoped for few anglers on this November day, but that didn't happen. Most of the parking spots had at least one car parked, and some had two or more. We weren't the only ones trying to take advantage of a beautiful fall day.

We eventually found an empty parking area, suited up, and walked the three minutes to the river. I cast upstream in very shallow water with an assortment of flies both on top and under the surface. We didn't see any action at all—no flashes, no bites, nothing. Norman assumed that the spot had been fished recently, thus putting down any fish for the next several hours.

I thought I could catch another Rio Grande cutthroat on the Pecos, but learned that these fish no longer inhabit the river except for above the mostly impassable Pecos Falls. In addition to over-harvesting by humans, an invasive species known as "rock snot," a contamination of the river due to mine tailings, and competition with other species changed just about everything on the river, forcing the Rio Grande cutthroat to leave their original habitat.

I fished north and south of the area known as the Pecos Box Canyon. The terrain is very different depending on where you fish. Below the Canyon, you can find an easily accessible river in meadow-like areas, but there you also find lots of anglers. The more forested area, where we concentrated our fishing efforts, was at the upper end of the box canyon near Cowles.

Just below Cowles, there were a couple of small ponds that Norman and I used to improve my long-distance casts. What exactly is a long-distance cast? A 60-70 foot cast is really good in my book, but just for comparison's sake, the long-distance competitive casting record is 248 feet according to globalflyfisher.com! It's much more important to have a long-distance cast when fishing in saltwater, but nevertheless, I would love to have a reliable 50-foot cast. I tried to focus on the movement of my arm and feel of the cast. Can you imagine how frustrating it must be to teach a novice when you are a competitive angler? Norman never let on—but he was a hard-driving teacher. We must have cast for 20-30 minutes before we walked over to some nearby holes on the river where I worked hard to find a few rainbows.

Norman wanted to drive downriver to private property where he had access. We left the two-lane paved road and drove down a long dirt lane that was partitioned by two gates prior to coming to a weathered cottage that sat about 15 yards from the river. We drove a little farther and parked the truck. Here was a setting for a great western novel.

Kelly Shannon owned the property, and we soon spotted him feeding the trout downstream, much like I feed the birds in my backyard. Kelly was a gentle soul and shared stories about his life on the river for decades. He pointed out various bends and curves where the river had changed due to active spring runoffs or other weather-related occurrences.

We saw fish in every expected spot in this stretch. It didn't take a particularly good cast or any special flies to hook one fish after another. The fish had not experienced dozens of

daily anglers, and they eagerly and undiscerningly ate most of the flies thrown at them. It was a great end to the fishing that day. As I parted with Norman, I wished him good luck with his upcoming World Fly-Fishing competition.

Traveling back to my campground in Santa Fe, I was treated to a beautiful New Mexican sunset. The sky turned a shimmering gray with layers of peach, pink, and gold while the clouds turned into flimsy wisps of pale purple. It made me yearn for a stretch of river property that would allow me to have my own daily ritual of feeding and watching over the fish and enjoying the enchanting sunsets. Now, that's pie in the sky.

San Juan River, New Mexico

December 2013

—

Again Really

—

San Juan River, New Mexico

The San Juan River is located in northwestern New Mexico in the Four Corners region where Colorado, New Mexico, Utah and Arizona meet. The river starts high in the San Juan Mountains in southwest Colorado and then travels through New Mexico and Utah before joining the Colorado on its way to Lake Powell. It is generally agreed that it's one of the top-ten tailwater fisheries in the country, for many reasons. First, fishing is possible throughout the entire year because of consistent 40-degree temperatures after the Navajo Dam. Next, the average size of a fish is between 17 to 19-inches or three to four pounds; and last, close to 60,000 fish exist in the first three miles after the dam.

In spite of all that juicy news, the fish on the San Juan can be extremely difficult to catch. I have fished there in three out of four seasons (not spring, when I hear the flows can be dangerously high) for a total of six times. I have never caught more than a couple of fish except the one time I fished in September in a drift boat with a guide from Duranglers, an outfitter located in nearby Durango, Colorado. Then I caught a dozen large fish. I think my success had more to do with having a guide than just a good day!

Conservationists have damned dams over the years, and in many situations, rightly so, but in the case of the San Juan, prior to the construction of the dam, the river was a silty, slow-moving stream, where catfish and suckers were the predominant fish. Obviously, the New Mexico Department of Game and Fish did an excellent job stocking the river with trout over the past 50 years, making it the fishery it is today.

Although I didn't fish the famous Texas Hole on this December trip to the San Juan, I should mention it because it is well known. Texas Hole is the deepest and fastest water in the river because three channels empty into this main hole. It is 200 yards of lots of fish and lots of anglers. It is not unusual to see an armada of drift boats circling the hole like a merry-go-round in their hunt for large rainbows. The one time I floated the San Juan, we spent about five minutes in Texas Hole before I asked to move on downriver because it simply wasn't the way I wanted to fish.

On this moderately cold December day, my husband and I left our home in Durango, heading south toward Navajo Lake, the body of water created by the Navajo Dam, which was dedicated in 1962. After the dam, the river flows through a colorful, austere, high-desert canyon. Like a postcard come to life, the sky here is inevitably a deep, rich blue. We decided to start fishing in the first half mile after the river emerges from the dam in the land of large rainbows, caught mostly with midges. The first ¼ mile is all catch and release, which is a good thing. Normally we would have stayed far away from these typically human-infested waters, but there was only one other angler, something almost unheard of on the San Juan.

I tied on a RS2 midge and a San Juan worm (of course) and hunted for those 17-inch rainbows for over an hour in various riffles and seams but didn't come up with anything. I decided to move to some of the braided areas of the river just a short distance downstream from us. Wading to the river's edge, I climbed the bank and made my way downstream. I scoped out a promising looking area with a large beaver dam. I think wood and fish are a magic combination.

It took me a while to make my way down to the river because I confronted a forest of willows that were so thick it was almost impossible to find a way through them. Every piece of clothing that I wore and equipment that hung from my body including my rod, net, fishing vest, hat, wading staff, and camera became entangled at one point or another in the trek to the river.

When I finally emerged from the willow jungle, I stayed close to the bank, thinking the wading would be easier, but it tended to slant down to the river, and an abundance of algae made it extremely slippery. I had a few slips through a cove that led to a point that I needed to get past to reach the run I had spotted before entering the willows. As I made my way around the point, I met up with a gaggle of Canada geese, which hissed at me and then threatened to charge me for having trespassed on their space. It surprised me, and I took a quick step backwards, hitting a branch that jetted out from the bank throwing me off balance. Down I went into the 40-degree water! Fortunately, I had done my reading about safety on a river and had tightly cinched up the belt on my waders, so I kept my legs dry. I escaped with only a wet jacket from the waist down. I sighed as I realized this was going to be another one of those challenging, but memorable fishing days.

I recomposed myself and headed up the last 50 yards to the run where I was sure I would be able to catch a fish. I tied a couple new flies including a size 20 brassie (1/8 of an inch)

onto my line followed by a zebra midge. My fingers were no longer nimble in 40-degree weather, but I finally got the job done with a lot of patience. I had heard about the 20-20 Club—a 20-inch fish on a size 20 hook—and thought that would be a cool club to join. I started casting to the run, which followed a beaver dam just upriver. My hunch was that the fish would be hanging out pretty close to the dam so that if they felt threatened, they had a nearby retreat. I knew it would be a tricky cast for me; I needed to land it close to the wood debris, but if I landed it too close, my flies would be history. I tried to be strategic by casting short to gauge how much line to cast, and I did pretty well for about ten minutes. Then, I noticed the Canada geese had made their way upriver closer to me, and I became momentarily distracted by their presence. My next cast went right onto the log, and there was no way I was going to retrieve my flies. I lost the whole rig including most of the leader, which would occupy my time for the next 15 minutes.

When I finished re-rigging, I decided to approach the riffle from a slightly different angle and made my way upriver a little closer to the beaver dam. I had been casting to the near side of the run but decided to take my chances on the far side, although the drift would be difficult with the faster water in between my flies and me. In the meantime, I noticed Florian coming around the point just north of the beaver dam. I started casting again and worked hard to mend my line to produce a good drift.

About 20 yards before Florian reached me, I felt a gentle tug on my line and knew I had a fish—now that's an impressive thing to do in front of an audience! I assumed the fish was one of the smaller ones in the San Juan because it didn't give me any fight as I reeled it in; however, as soon as I had it within 20 feet I could see it was one of those famous 17 to 19-inch San Juan rainbows. At the same time I netted it, Florian arrived to observe my prize. As I reached in the net to pick up the fish and remove the hook, it looked up at both of us as if to say, "Really? How could this have happened again?" It had a gash on its head from a heron attack, and its mouth had definite signs of previous hook-ups. At first I snickered at the fish's reaction, but then I felt incredibly bad for the life this fish had been handed—dodging hooks and predators. I gently released it back to the river, wishing it good luck in avoiding the dangers of its life in the San Juan. I guess all living creatures have their challenges to face—I certainly do.

Animas River, Colorado

216

December 2013

Yatta

Animas River, Colorado

In the early 2000s, I worked as a public services librarian and an adjunct professor in French and writing at Fort Lewis College in Durango, Colorado. This was a dream job for me—living in a mountain town in Colorado and working at a small liberal arts college. I thought I had found the place where I would live out the rest of my life. Unfortunately, the job didn't work out, so I moved on to another in Denver, but kept the Durango townhouse we owned. Once my husband and I are both retired, we hope to spend a lot more time there. Durango is a place where dreams are made—there's nothing you can't be or do there—cowboy, rancher, gambler, hiker, biker, writer, skier, photographer, artist or angler. Although I'm not part of the .01 percent, I am certainly fortunate to be able to live in two great places in such a magnificent state.

The Animas River, like many Western rivers, suffered from abusive practices for decades. Mine tailings and sewage were regularly dumped into the river, and it wasn't until the mid-1990s that the Animas River Stakeholders formed to see that the Animas users comply with provisions of the Clean Water Act. Now, 20 years beyond that, I don't think many would argue that the Animas is as nice a river as any to fish.

From my townhouse's kitchen window, I am privy to a little bit of Americana every day as the Durango & Silverton Narrow Gauge Railroad chugs its way along Highway 550 on a spectacular 45-mile trip to the historic mining town of Silverton, Colorado. I've made the round trip once—with my husband, two sons and one of their spouses. It's an all-day commitment (unless you opt for the bus ride back from Silverton) taking you through beautiful country on a 36-inch track along stunning mountain slopes. Quite remarkable!

I can walk down to the Animas River from our Durango home that's located eight miles north of town, although I'm not allowed to fish there because the land is private. To fish the Animas, I need to head back to town where there are several easily accessible spots. In fact, over two miles of "Gold Medal" stream are located just a short walk from downtown Durango. (For Gold Medal designation by the Colorado Wildlife Commission, a river must contain at least 60 pounds of trout per acre of water, plus there must be at least 12 quality trout, 16 inches or longer.) Even though I have had a place in Durango for 13 years, I am embarrassed to say I only fished the river twice. Just driven by different priorities, I guess.

I have fished several other rivers around Durango, including the Pine, the Piedra and the San Juan, which is 40 minutes to the south over the New Mexico border (see Chapter 50). Our subdivision is also quite special in that all homeowners own some miniscule amount of water rights from the Animas River, which feeds ponds and waterways throughout the subdivision. My husband loves to say that he can stand on our deck, cast a woolly bugger and serve up a rainbow trout for lunch—and that's not too far from the truth.

After fishing in New Mexico, I settled in at our home in Durango for a couple of weeks. I was nearing the end of my epic adventure and I used the time to organize recent photos and write my heart out. Like the rest of the country, the weather was cold with highs only in the 30s. I kept waiting for a warmer day to fish, but that didn't happen. After all the cold fishing days I had experienced earlier in the year, I felt rather wimpy at this juncture.

Florian had driven down from Denver to Durango to fish the San Juan with me and stayed for the Animas. (He has fished the Animas dozens of times over the last 30 years.) It was 25 degrees when we arrived at the first fishing hole. The

Animas is wide and easily accessible throughout town—just park your car and walk 20 feet and you're in the river. The trees were covered with hoarfrost crystals and the bank of the river was iced up, making it tricky to find solid ground from which to a cast. The bottom of the river is mostly cobblestone and thus very slippery.

With walking staffs in hand and waders tightly belted, we headed in different directions and didn't meet back up again until the end of the day to compare stories. There are lots of jokes about husbands and wives fishing together and the stress that causes, but I have to say, we have done really well by each going our own way. It's just that he likes to say he caught one more fish than I!

My fly selection was typical for this time of year—small nymphs and midges and, oh yes, the good ol' woolly bugger streamers. I tied on size 22 copper johns and zebra midges and remarked at how simple it seemed in comparison to just 12 months ago. These flies are only about 1/16th of an inch, so it takes a lot of practice to learn how to thread and tie a knot with a hair-sized section of monofilament line to the eye of the hooks. I had hoped to see a blue winged olive hatch, but I pushed the envelope on that wish.

I fished the edges of the faster riffles, the pools behind the large boulders, the far banks and the runs in the middle of the river, but the fish expressed no interest. After a good six hours of fishing, I signaled to my husband that it was time to dine at Season's, one of our favorite restaurants in Durango.

The dinner was a sort of celebration for having completed my year of fishing 52 rivers, although I felt ambivalent about the experience ending. I expected to become tired of it all and to yearn for the comforts of my home, but that never happened. In fact, if family obligations and money were not issues, I might have just kept on going! However, I realized that if I continued on the same path, I would be so busy fishing, meeting people, taking photos, and traveling, that I would not have time to write my book.

Writing the book was my inspiration to return home. I couldn't keep this year of discovery to myself. I had to share it and inspire others to follow their dreams. I have always loved Joseph Campbell's expression, "Follow Your Bliss." I did that.

Writing the book was my inspiration to return home. I couldn't keep this year of discovery to myself.

On the last day, on the last river of this journey, I visited the Animas at the north end of town. There, the river changes a bit. Humongous boulders create odd currents and make it hard to read the water. I fished during the morning and once again, came up empty handed. In the afternoon, I shot photos finding synchronicity between photography and fly-fishing. There were many times throughout the year I thought I should just focus on photography and not the fishing, but that's only when I came up empty-handed with the rod. I loved being able to document with photographs the joys of fly-fishing and the gorgeous surroundings where fish live. On my drive home, Mother Nature gifted me with a beautiful display of some lenticular clouds that were a sign to me that I had many more photographs to take in many new locations. And, many more rivers to fish.

Glossary

Bounce rig

A fishing rig with the weight on the bottom of the leader with two short droppers above.

CFS (cubic feet per second)

A unit of measurement expressing the rate of discharge (or rate of flow) of water. One cubic foot per second equals 448.8 gallons per minute.

Dry flies

Flies that anglers use to fish on the water surface. An angler can actually observe the fish taking the fly.

Dropper

One fly attached behind another fly. Often is attached to the bend of the hook or leader. http://www.skatethefly.com/learn/glossary.asp

Flies

(partial listing mentioned in the book) Some of these are categories of flies and some double as the insect's name.

Baetis	Purple Haze
Brassie	Renegade
Chubby chernobyl	Royal Wolff
Golden stonefly	San Juan Worm
Green (or brown) drake	Sculpin
Hackle stacker	Stimulator
Hare's ear	Stonefly
Mayfly	Streamer
Parachute adams	Ugly bug
PMD	Wooly Bugger
Pheasant tail	Zebra Midge

Freestone Rivers

Rivers that have a significant gradient resulting in medium to fast-moving water and the water usually comes from runoff or tributaries. They are so-named for the rock and gravel that make up their riverbed. (www.orvis.com)

Fry

The stage in the life of a trout when it will act like a fish for the first time and start to emerge from the rocks and swim.

Hawgs

A large fish with a wide girth.

Indicator

Floating object placed on the leader or end of the fly line to "indicate" the take of the fly by a fish or to indicate the path of the drift of the fly.

Jig rig

A pivotal hook and slim-profile weight; mostly used for bait fishing.

Leader

The section of fishing line between the reel's fly line and the fly.

Mend(ing)

A technique that is used after a fishing line is on the water to achieve a drag free float by slowing down the speed of the line as it travels downstream. (www.orvis.com)

Nymphs

The immature form of insects.

Piscatorial

Of or concerning fisherman or fishing.

Piscivorous

Of an animal feeding on fish.

Redd

A spawning nest made by a fish, especially a salmon or trout.

Riffle

A rocky or shallow part of a stream or river with rough water, usually at either end of a pool.

Rise

The action of a fish at the water's surface when eating.

Seam line of water

The area where two current flows come together—ideal for holding fish. (www.redington.com)

Strip

Retrieve the line by pulling it through your fingers as opposed to winding it in by the reel.

Tailwater

The downstream section of a river or stream found below a large man-made dam. (www.redington.com)

Thingamabobber

A kind of indicator used on a fishing line when fishing.

Tippet

The end section of a leader that the fly is tied to.

Took the skunk off

Caught your first fish of the day.

Yatta

Yatta is a Japanese short form for "yari-mashita," which translates to "(I/We) did it!" or "it's done!"

Guides

Jeremy Allan

riverdazeglx@msn.com
801.638.6263

Strawberry River, Provo River, UT

Rob Burden

Steamboat Flyfisher
rob@steamboatflyfisher.com
970.879.6552

Yampa River, CO

Leslie Dal Lago

Reel-Woman Fly Fish Adventures
lesdallago@hotmail.com
208-221-5475

Henry's Fork, ID

Pat Dorsey

Blue Quill Angler
flyfish@bluequillangler.com
303.674.4700

South Platte, Cheesman, CO

Angus Drummond

Black Canyon Anglers
info@blackcanyonanglers.com
970.835.5050

Gunnison, Black Canyon, CO

Bill Dvorak

Dvorak Expeditions
bill@dvorakexpeditions.com
719.539.6851

Arkansas River, CO

Kirk Gammill

Montana Flyfishing Connection
Kirkgammill@hotmail.com
406.370.2868

Smith River, MT

Dave Hill

San Miguel Anglers
www.sanmiguelanglers.com
970-728-4477

Dolores, San Miguel, CO

Natalie Jensen / Terry Gunn

Lee's Ferry Anglers
www.leesferryanglers.com
928.355.2261

Colorado River, AZ

John Huber

Picabo Angler
john@picaboangler.com
208.788.3536

Silver Creek, Little Wood, ID

David Hufman

Grizzly Hackle Fly Shop
info@grizzlyhackle.com
406.721.8996

Blackfoot, MT

Derek Hutton

World Cast Anglers
Derek@silverstar.com
208.399.1888

N. Platte, Snake, WY. Henry's Fork, ID

Mike Kelly

Kingfisher Lodge
www.bighornkingfisher.com
406.666.2326

Bighorn River, MT

Paul Killino

Colorado River Outfitters
paul@coloradoriveroutfitters.com
970.653.FISH

Colorado, Lake Fork of the Gunnison, CO

Bob Krumm

Blue Quill Fly Company
rkrumm@fiberpipe.net
406.666.2229

Bighorn River, MT

Norman Maktima

High Desert Angler
www.highdesertangler.com
505.470.0405

Pecos River, NM

Jack Mauer

Wapiti Waters Fly Fishing Montana
wapiti@wapiti-waters.com
406.642.6548

Bitterroot River, MT

Joe Moore

Big Sky Anglers
joe@bigskyanglers.com
406.581.6059

Madison River, MT

Ryan Newman

Rocky Mountain Outfitters
mo.reservations@gmail.com
435.654.1655

Provo River, UT

Russell Parks

The Missoulian Angler
fly-shop@missoulianangler.com
406.728.7766

Bitterroot River, Rock Creek, MT

Jared Edens / Mark Raisler

Headhunters Fly Shop
info@headhuntersflyshop.com
406.235.3447

Missouri River, MT

Troy Smith

Conejos River Anglers
Conejosanglers@gmail.com
719.376.5660

Conejos River, CO

Nick Streit

Taos Fly Shop and The Reel Life
info@taosflyshop.com
575.751.1312

Rio Grande Gorge, Red River,
Cimarron River, Chama River, NM

Tony Valeriano

westerndrifters.com
406.223.7364

Yellowstone River, MT

Afterword

I set goals for my year of *52 Rivers* that I'm close to completing as I write this final section of my book. Some of the goals were straight forward—travel to 52 rivers and fish them. Some were intangible—inspire others to follow their passion, while others were paltry—learn how to tie some knots. Goals gave me clarity and focus, drove me forward to do the best I could and made me accountable.

When I first started talking about the idea for this project, my friends said, "I didn't even know you fly-fished!" And they weren't far from the truth. This was about so much more than fly-fishing. I recall author Nick Lyons' precept of fly-fishing that surmised that the best fly-fishing books weren't really about fly-fishing, they were about the stories. From the start I wanted to tell stories—about the people I met, the places I visited, and what I learned about fly-fishing along the way—never claiming to be a guru on the subject. I believe I've accomplished that goal.

I was asked about what I did with the fish I caught. Did I kill them? Eat them? I followed the practice of catch and release. I didn't keep any fish all year, and I was careful to make sure they were able to swim away. Catch and release is not without its controversies, but it worked for me.

And so the adventure ends, just like the seasons and cycles of nature. I feel a bit melancholy as I do sometimes when fall passes into winter. I am grateful for all that I have learned and seen. I understand more about patience, humility, challenges, changes and life and death. On the stream and in the wild, the different seasons showed me the many faces of the natural course of events. Some people who were with me at the start of my journey are no longer here—my good friend, Carol Dorfman, Andy Buck, father and friend, Bob Lay, fellow angler and my father, Robert Brightman. Throughout the trip I met so many people and found new life with my grandson, Maxwell.

I love Shel Silverstein's children's book, *The Story of Lafcadio: The Lion Who Shot Back*. A lion is the protagonist in the book, and he wants a new identity, finds one, doesn't like it but doesn't know what to do next. The book ends with this rather philosophical comment: "And he didn't really know what was going to happen to him, but he did know that something was going to happen, because something always does, doesn't it?"

I don't know what's next for me, but I do know something is going to happen.